Anxiety Disorders Comorbid with Depression:
Panic disorder and agoraphobia

Anxiety Disorders Comorbid with Depression: Panic disorder and agoraphobia

David Nutt, FRCPsych
Adrian Feeney, MRCPsych and
Spilios Argyropolous, MRCPsych

Psychopharmacology Unit
The School of Medical Sciences
Bristol University
Bristol
UK

MARTIN DUNITZ

© 2002 Martin Dunitz Ltd, a member of
the Taylor & Francis group

First published in the United Kingdom
in 2002 by
Martin Dunitz Ltd
The Livery House
7–9 Pratt Street
London NW1 0AE

Tel: +44 (0)207 482 2202
Fax: +44 (0)207 267 0159
E-mail: info.dunitz@tandf.co.uk
Website: http://www.dunitz.co.uk

A CIP catalogue record for this book is
available from the British Library

ISBN 1-84184-049-1

Distributed in the USA by:
Fulfilment Centre, Taylor & Francis, 7625 Empire Drive, Florence, KY41042, USA
Toll free Tel: +1 800 634 7064   E-mail: cserve@routledge_ny.com

Distributed in Canada by:
Taylor & Francis, 74 Rolark Drive, Scarborough, Ontario, M1R 4G2, Canada
Toll free Tel: +1 877 226 2237   E-mail: tal_fran@istar.ca

Distributed in the rest of the world by:
ITPS Limited, Cheriton House, North Way, Andover, Hampshire, SP10 5BE, UK
Tel: +44 (0) 1264 332424   E-mail: reception@itps.co.uk

Printed and bound in Italy by Printer Trento S.r.l.

Contents

Panic disorder and agoraphobia: an historical introduction

It has been argued that the recognition of anxiety disorders in the early nineteenth century can be seen in the context of the reduced level of threat in society in general. It was only in the affluent and more predictable conditions of the industrial developed world that these symptoms can be seen as an abnormal response to a relatively unthreatening world. In these less threatening conditions, the minority who experience ongoing nervousness and paroxysmal anxiety attacks were then identified as worthy of treatment. Before that, anxiety had not been perceived as a mental illness in its own right, rather more as a social stress and a possible cause of mental illness (Berrios and Link 1995).

Anxiety symptoms throughout the nineteenth and into the first half of the twentieth centuries were often described within the medical model on an individual basis, related to their presentation (Da Costa described irritable heart, Lewis effort syndrome and Oppenheimer the neurocirculatory syndrome). Westphal also incorrectly used the medical model to explain 'platzschwindel', which has since been renamed agoraphobia. He mistakenly identified this inability to cross open spaces unaccompanied as an abnormality of the sense of balance resulting from inner-ear pathology. Later, Legrand du Saulle refined this concept by correctly identifying that the sufferer did in fact have a fear of losing his balance rather than an actual balance problem (Berrios and Link 1995). The development of theories of aetiology of anxiety brought about the recognition that these various system-based syndromes were manifestations of the autonomic symptoms of anxiety.

In 1880, Beard, a distinguished North American neurologist, proposed the existence of neurasthenia or mental exhaustion. This was characterized by severe tiredness of sudden onset in the absence of organic abnormality, which was speculated to be caused by the increasingly frenetic pace of life in an industrialized country. The American psychiatric community enthusiastically adopted this diagnosis. Some 15 years later, Freud (1953) published his paper separating anxiety neurosis from neurasthenia. Morbid anxiety, i.e. anxiety in the absence of external threat, was the basis of this separation. Originally, Freud suggested that the anxiety neurosis was a manifestation of undischarged libidinal energy. Freud clearly described panic attacks in this paper. He noted that panic attacks were unpredictable, often lacked an identifiable precipitant, and were associated with certain cognitions and somatic symptoms. He made no effort to separate panic attacks from anxiety neurosis. Freud's influence over the categorization of anxiety was still clearly evident in the *Diagnostic and Statistical Manual of Mental Disorders*, 3rd edition (DSM-III) (American Psychiatric Association 1980).

Later the concept of neurosis was removed from DSM-IV (American Psychiatric Association 1994) because of the atheoretical stance that this diagnostic manual took. The concept of anxiety neurosis being the product of intrapsychic conflict could not be substantiated. The current diagnostic category of panic disorder in DSM-IV is largely the result of the work of Klein. In the early 1960s, Klein and Fink treated a variety of psychiatric inpatients with the tricyclic antidepressant imipramine. They noted that patients who had anxiety neurosis underwent a very selective improvement in their symptoms. Imipramine successfully alleviated their panic attacks without having any effect on their levels of background anxiety. However, in contrast, low-dose benzodiazepine treatment did not cause this improvement in panic attacks, although it did reduce the background anxiety. They speculated that the panic attacks were the product of a separate neural circuit to the background anxiety and that, when panic attacks occurred in a spontaneous fashion, they could usefully be described as the basis of a separate condition – panic disorder (Klein 1964). This pharmacological dissection of panic disorder, as Klein described it, is not as clear-cut as his initial studies suggest. It is now recognized that panic disorder does indeed respond to benzodiazepines, but at higher doses than Klein used. Later, Klein (1981) suggested that, rather than panic attacks being the fruit of anxiety, they were the cause via conditioning of the avoidance behaviour agoraphobia.

The DSM-IV system of classification embraces this view and classifies agoraphobia as secondary to panic disorder. The *International Classification of Mental and Behavioural Disorders*, 10th revision (ICD-10) is more sceptical and has a primary diagnosis of agoraphobia with or without panic attacks (WHO 1992).

Diagnosis, classification, epidemiology and comorbidity of panic disorder and agoraphobia

Classification of panic disorder and agoraphobia

The anxiety disorders chapter in the DSM-IV is organized around the concept of the panic attack. It recognizes that such attacks can occur in all of the anxiety disorders in certain circumstances. It also states that spontaneous panic attacks are characteristic of panic disorder itself. DSM-IV also defines agoraphobia as a diagnosis secondary to panic disorder after the theories of Klein (see earlier).

A panic attack is an episode of intense anxiety that has associated somatic and cognitive symptoms (Table 1). To fulfil the criteria for a panic attack, at least 4 of the 13 symptoms must be present. If fewer than four symptoms are displayed, it is called a limited symptom attack.

Panic attacks may be uncued (characteristic of panic disorder), situationally bound (in specific phobias and social phobia) and situationally predisposed (may occur in panic disorder, social phobia or specific phobia). Panic attacks that are perceived as unpredictable are invariably accompanied by feelings of loss of control and dizziness, which is presumably because, in the face of inexplicable symptoms, the individual does feel out of control. It is worth emphasizing that the unpredictable nature of these uncued episodes of fearfulness is a cornerstone of the diagnosis of panic disorder. A further discussion regarding this statement is included in the section about the debate on the existence of panic disorder in the next chapter.

A discrete period of intense fear or discomfort, in which four (or more) of the following symptoms developed abruptly and reached a peak within 10 minutes:

1. Palpitations, pounding heart or accelerated heart rate
2. Sweating
3. Trembling or shaking
4. Sensations of shortness of breath or smothering
5. Feeling of choking
6. Chest pain or discomfort
7. Nausea or abdominal distress
8. Feeling dizzy, unsteady, light-headed or faint
9. Derealization (feelings of unreality) or depersonalization (being detached from oneself)
10. Fear of losing control or going crazy
11. Fear of dying
12. Paraesthesia (numbness or tingling sensations)
13. Chills or hot flushes

Table 1
DSM-IV criteria for panic attack

The diagnosis of agoraphobia is intimately linked to panic disorder in DSM-IV. Agoraphobia is defined as anxiety that occurs in situations in which escape is difficult or embarrassing, or in which help would be unavailable in the event of a panic attack (Table 2). It is, however, possible to make the diagnosis of agoraphobia without a history of panic disorder.

A Anxiety about being in places or situations from which escape might be difficult (or embarrassing) or in which help may not be available in the event of having an unexpected or situationally predisposed panic attack or panic-like symptoms. Agoraphobia fears typically involve characteristic clusters of situations that include being outside the home alone; being in a crowd or standing in a line; being on a bridge; and travelling in a bus, train or automobile.

Note: consider the diagnosis of specific phobia if the avoidance is limited to one or only a few specific situations, or social phobia if the avoidance is limited to social situations.

B The situations are avoided (e.g. travel is restricted) or else are endured with marked distress or with anxiety about having a panic attack or panic-like symptoms, or require the presence of a companion.

C The anxiety or phobic avoidance is not better accounted for by another mental disorder, such as social phobia (e.g. avoidance limited to social situations because of fear of embarrassment), specific phobia (e.g. avoidance limited to a single situation such as elevators or lifts), obsessive–compulsive disorder (e.g. avoidance of dirt in someone with an obsession about contamination), post- traumatic stress disorder (e.g. avoidance of stimuli associated with a severe stressor) or separation anxiety disorder (e.g. avoidance of leaving home or relatives).

Table 2
DSM-IV criteria for agoraphobia

The essential feature of panic disorder, according to the DSM-IV, is the presence of recurrent, unexpected panic attacks. There is no specification of the precise frequency of panic attacks to fulfil the criteria for panic disorder in DSM-IV. At least one of the attacks has to be followed by one month or more of the following: persistent concern about having a further attack, worry about the consequences of having an attack or a significant change in behaviour (Table 3). Besides this worry about further panic attacks, there may also be unfocused anxiety present between attacks. At least two of the panic attacks have to be spontaneous (uncued or 'out of the blue') for a diagnosis of panic disorder to be made. However, situationally predisposed panic attacks are also common in panic disorder.

Within the criteria for panic disorder, it is stipulated that the panic attacks should not be accounted for better by another anxiety disorder. However, DSM-IV is not hierarchical and does allow the diagnosis of two anxiety disorders simultaneously if the criteria for each are met independently.

The fundamental component of the neurotic and stress-related disorders found in the ICD-10 is the concept of phobia. A phobia is a disorder characterized by anxiety provoked by specific situations or objects that are not inherently dangerous, leading to avoidance. Thus, unlike the DSM-IV, agoraphobia is the primary diagnosis that is classified as being with or without panic attacks. Furthermore, ICD-10 is hierarchical and the phobias, agoraphobia (Table 4), social phobia and specific phobia take precedence over panic disorder. If social phobia is complicated by panic attacks, it is coded in ICD-10 as social phobia and the panic attacks are presumed to be merely an expression of the severity of the social phobia.

A   Both (1) and (2)

    (1)   recurrent unexpected panic attacks;
    (2)   at least one of the attacks has been followed by 1 month (or more) of one (or more) of the following:

        (a)   persistent concern about having additional attacks;
        (b)   worry about the implications of the attack or its consequences (e.g. losing control, having a heart attack, 'going crazy');
        (c)   a significant change in behaviour related to the attacks.

B   Presence/absence of agoraphobia;

C   The panic attacks are not due to the direct physiological effects of a substance (e.g. a drug of abuse, a medication) or a general medical condition (e.g. hyperthyroidism);

D   The panic attacks are not better accounted for by another mental disorder, such as social phobia (e.g. occurring on exposure to feared social situations), specific phobia (e.g. on exposure to a specific phobic situation), obsessive–compulsive disorder (e.g. on exposure to dirt in someone with an obsession about contamination), post-traumatic stress disorder (e.g. in response to stimuli associated with a severe stressor) or separation anxiety disorder (e.g. in response to being away from home or close relatives).

Table 3
DSM-IV diagnostic criteria for panic disorder with/without agoraphobia

All of the following should be fulfilled for a definite diagnosis:

A The psychological or autonomic symptoms must be primarily manifestations of anxiety and not secondary to other symptoms, such as delusions or obsessional thoughts;

B The anxiety must be restricted to (or occur mainly in) at least two of the following situations: crowds, public places, travelling away from home and travelling alone, and

C Avoidance of the phobic situation must be, or have been, a prominent feature.

Table 4
ICD-10 diagnostic guidelines for agoraphobia

Panic disorder (Table 5) in ICD-10 has a more peripheral role than in DSM-IV. ICD-10 stipulates that several episodes of intense anxiety with associated autonomic symptoms must occur within a 1-month period, that these should be spontaneous and that there should be relative freedom from anxiety between panic attacks.

In this classification, a panic attack that occurs in an established phobic situation is regarded as an expression of the severity of the phobia, which should be given diagnostic precedence. Panic disorder should be the main diagnosis only in the absence of any of the phobic anxiety disorders (agoraphobia, social phobia and specific [isolated] phobia).

For a definitive diagnosis, several severe attacks of autonomic anxiety should have occurred within a period of about 1 month:

A   in circumstances where there is no objective danger;

B   without being confined to known or predictable situations, and

C   with comparative freedom from anxiety symptoms between attacks (although anticipatory anxiety is common).

Table 5
ICD-10 diagnostic guidelines for panic disorder (episodic paroxysmal anxiety)

Symptoms associated with panic disorder

The recurrent panic attacks of panic disorder are often accompanied by the following symptoms: anticipatory anxiety, hypochondriasis and demoralization.

Anticipatory anxiety

Anticipatory anxiety is the result of the fear of the next attack occurring. This ongoing anxiety may present with hyperactivity and apprehension, and may be confused with the free-floating anxiety seen in generalized anxiety disorder (GAD).

Hypochondriasis

Panic disorder patients often present the autonomic symptoms of their attacks to doctors in primary care or accident and emergency (A&E) departments. In the complex mix of psychological and autonomic symptoms, it is possible for the latter to take precedence and for the patient to become preoccupied with their cause. Thus, they develop secondary hypochondriasis (a concern that they have a serious disease based on their incorrect interpretation that their autonomic symptoms are the result of a serious physical disease).

Barsky et al (1994) screened consecutive patients in a primary care setting for panic disorder. They identified 100 patients who met DSM-III criteria for panic disorder; of these, 25 also met the criteria for hypochondriasis. Noyes et al (1986) showed that the level of hypochondriacal symptoms in patients with panic disorder and agoraphobia was reduced by successful treatment of the somatic symptoms of anxiety.

Demoralization

Panic disorder can be debilitating, especially if complicated by agoraphobia. Individuals who have had their level of functioning markedly reduced are vulnerable to unhappiness, and there is a strong association between panic disorder and depression (see page 59).

Differential diagnosis

Panic disorder may be mimicked by the anxiety disorders listed in Table 6. Panic attacks that are secondary to a medical condition will have a close temporal relationship with that medical condition. Substance misuse can cause panic attacks, either by intoxication with stimulants or by withdrawal from depressants.

Anxiety resulting from medical conditions

- Hyperthyroidism
- Hyperparathyroidism
- Phaeochromocytoma
- Seizure disorders
- Vestibular dysfunction
- Cardiac conditions (arrhythmias and supraventricular dysfunction)

Substance-induced anxiety disorders

- Cocaine
- Amphetamine   } Intoxication with stimulants
- Caffeine

- Cannabis
- Alcohol   } Withdrawal from depressants
- Barbiturates

Anxiety disorders

- Social phobia
- Specific phobia
- Obsessive–compulsive disorder
- Post-traumatic distress disorder

Separation anxiety

Psychotic disorders

Table 6
Anxiety disorders

Medical comorbidity

Panic disorder has been found to have an association with a variety of medical conditions. This may be the result of patients with panic disorder presenting their symptoms more readily to the doctor. The presence of comorbid medical conditions may increase the severity of symptoms and worsen the prognosis of panic disorder. All the conditions in the upper section of Table 6 may be comorbid with panic disorder, and make it more difficult to make an accurate diagnosis. Thus, although it is important for the physician to consider the diagnosis of panic disorder in a patient presenting with a variety of physical symptoms, it is equally important for the psychiatrist to consider the physical diseases that mimic panic disorder.

Patients with panic disorder have increased cardiovascular morbidity and mortality (Weisman et al 1990). This observation may result from the strong association of panic disorder with depression, which has a recognized association with cardiovascular disease. However, the association may also be the result of the relationship between a poorer cardiovascular risk profile and panic disorder (smoking, alcohol dependence, lack of exercise and social isolation). Panic disorder patients also present with arrhythmias, which can be caused by increased sensitivity to their own physiological symptoms (see page 36). Commonly, the arrhythmia is sinus tachycardia.

Mitral valve prolapse (MVP) is a condition that effects about 5% of the population. It has been reported that MPV is more common in those who have panic disorder and that panic disorder is common in those who have MPV. However, patients with panic disorder form an unusual group, who are likely to be extremely vigilant about cardiac symptoms. This may well cause a bias, with more panic disorder patients presenting with cardiac symptoms, and therefore being diagnosed with MPV. In fact, when MPV patients are compared with other cardiac patients, there is no difference in the prevalence of panic disorder in the two groups. The association between panic disorder and mitral valve may therefore be spurious (Jake and Taylor 1999).

An association of panic disorder with pulmonary disease would be intriguing in light of Klein's theory that an over-sensitive suffocation alarm is responsible for panic attacks (see page 48). However, the studies to date have proved inconclusive. The Epidemiological Catchment Area (ECA) study (Walker et al 1992) has shown an association between those who have gastrointestinal symptoms and lifetime risk of both panic disorder (a 3.5 times increased risk) and depression (a 2.5 times increased risk).

Vestibular disorders presenting with dizziness and vertigo can also be confused with panic disorder. There is only a small amount of evidence that such disorders are more common in panic disorder.

Panic disorder patients have higher rates of physical illness than normal controls. On the one hand, this may result from the poorer cardiac risk profile associated with panic disorder or the possibility of respiratory disease interacting with the abnormally sensitive suffocation alarm, and on the other, the association with comorbid physical illness probably results partly from the increased vigilance by the patients for their symptoms, leading them to present more readily to their doctors.

Epidemiology of panic attacks and panic disorder

Since the separate diagnosis of panic disorder was created in 1980 in DSM-III, it has been the subject of much epidemiological research to establish its prevalence internationally. With the proviso that the prevalence studies for panic disorder employ a variety of diagnostic interviews and diagnostic criteria for panic disorder (DSM-III, DSM-IIIR, DSM-I) it is remarkable that the lifetime prevalence of panic disorder itself is consistent in different studies (Weisman et al 1997) (Figure 1). This is not the case for panic attacks and may reflect the greater consistency of the diagnosis of panic disorder as a result of its more stringent criteria.

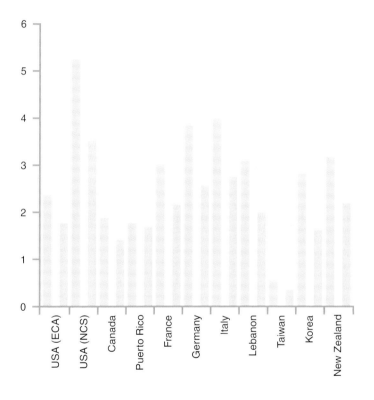

Figure 1
Prevalence rates of panic disorder per 100 in community-based surveys (Weissman et al 1997). (Green: Women; blue: men; violet: total.)

Demography

Both the ECA (Eaton et al 1991) and the National Comorbidity Survey (NCS) (Eaton et al 1994) have shown a bimodal distribution in the age at onset of panic disorder, the first peak of onset being in the age group of 15–24 years and the second in the age group 45–54 years.

Figure 1 demonstrates that in all the studies listed, the prevalence of panic disorder was greater in women than in men. This difference was a significant one in all except the studies from Taiwan and Puerto Rico. However, it appears that this sex difference is largely the result of the preponderance of women among those who have panic disorder with agoraphobia rather than panic disorder without agoraphobia.

People who have been educated for more than 16 years had a ten times smaller risk of having a panic disorder than those who had been educated for up to 12 years (Eaton et al 1994).

Other risk factors identified for panic disorder include being divorced or widowed, and living in an urban area rather than a rural one (Table 7).

- Female

- Divorced or separated

- Urban dwelling

- Fewer years of formal education

Table 7
Risk factors for panic disorder

Comorbidity

Panic disorder and agoraphobia

Both the Cross-National Collaborative study and the NCS have demonstrated a consistent association between panic disorder and agoraphobia. In the former, the odds ratio of panic disorder for those with agoraphobia ranged from 7.5 in the ECA to 21.4 in Puerto Rico. This is consistent with Klein's theory that agoraphobia is a secondary avoidance phenomenon triggered by the aversive experience of spontaneous panic attacks. However, several community surveys report that there are many individuals who have agoraphobia but no history of panic attacks.

Some have speculated that this is largely the result of under-diagnosis of panic disorder in these community surveys. Such under-diagnosis may be caused by the survey being carried out by lay-people using the diagnostic interview schedule (DIS) (Robins et al 1981). In clinical settings, clinicians diagnose panic disorder more frequently in the presence of agoraphobia than the lay-people used in community surveys. An alternative explanation is that comorbidity of agoraphobia and panic disorder is indeed more common in clinical settings than in the community.

The ECA study originally identified 22 cases of agoraphobia without panic attacks. However, when these cases were re-examined, it was found that 19 of the patients had incorrectly been diagnosed with agoraphobia and a further six had panic attacks that had been missed. Thus, the original data had over-estimated the prevalence of agoraphobia in the absence of panic disorder (Howarth et al 1993).

Agoraphobia appears to complicate panic disorder more frequently in women than in men. In fact, over three-quarters of those panic patients who manifest significant avoidance are women (Myres et al 1984). Table 8 shows the differences in the sex ratio between different groups of panic disorder patients. Women with panic disorder appear to be more prone to have comorbid depression (see page 66).

	Female	Male
Panic disorder without agoraphobia	1	1
Panic disorder with/without agoraphobia[a]	~3	1
Community sample of panic disorder with /without agoraphobia (ECA)	3	2

[a]This represents the mean of all the sex ratios in the Cross-National Epidemiology Study (Weissman et al 1997).

Table 8
Sex ratio of panic disorder with/without agoraphobia

What is the primary pathology of the panic attack/agoraphobia syndrome?

Klein hypothesized that the panic attack was fundamental to the aetiology of the panic disorder/agoraphobia syndrome (Klein 1981). He suggested that spontaneous unprovoked panic attacks evolved into cued attacks, triggering anticipatory anxiety which, in turn, led to the avoidance behaviour manifested in agoraphobia. There is a wide variety of evidence supporting the biological nature of panic attacks.

Klein's theory does not explain why some patients present with agoraphobia in the absence of panic disorder. This tends to support the European view that the primary pathology in those anxiety disorders presenting with panic attacks is the phobia. Thus, although the attacks are perceived to be spontaneous and without a precipitant, there are probably subtle unnoticed phobic triggers for the attack.

Panic disorder and the other anxiety disorders (Table 9)

The rates for comorbidity of panic disorder are high. The ECA study showed that almost 50% of patients with a history of an anxiety disorder had a lifetime risk of at least one other comorbid anxiety disorder. Thus, panic attacks that meet the criteria for panic disorder are common among other anxiety disorders. Indeed, Freud described how panic rose from the volcanic sea of anxiety.

Primary diagnosis	Percentage with comorbid panic disorder	Reference
Agoraphobia	29.5–58.2	Weissman et al 1997
Social phobia	19.2–73.9	
Generalized anxiety disorder	20	Goisman et al 1994
Obsessive–compulsive disorder	14	
Post-traumatic stress disorder	6	

Table 9
Comorbidity

As mentioned earlier, the ICD-10 classification system is hierarchical and therefore does not allow for comorbid anxiety disorders. There are some instances where it can be quite difficult to tease out which anxiety disorder is predominant. Thus, for a patient who has a severe social phobia and does not leave his home for fear of meeting people, agoraphobia is given precedence.

The temporal relationship between panic disorder and other comorbid psychiatric conditions appears to be an area of controversy. Faravelli and Paionni (1999) comment that, apart from depression and alcohol dependence, other conditions seldom develop after the onset of panic disorder. Tyrer (1984), on the other hand, has suggested that panic disorder can be usefully seen as 'a common station along the track to other neurotic stations'.

Panic disorder and generalized anxiety disorder (GAD)

Is there a difference between panic disorder and GAD?

Tyrer (1984) has argued that the creation of the separate diagnostic entity of panic disorder necessitated the simultaneous creation of the complementary diagnosis GAD (Table 10). Assuming this premise to be correct, GAD was characterized by unfocused anxiety and worry in the absence of panic attacks. It is now recognized that high-dose benzodiazepines are effective in treating panic attacks if given at adequate doses. Klein's original contention that panic attacks represented a separate entity was based on his work with relatively low doses of benzodiazepines. Thus, this piece of evidence for the existence of the separate condition, panic disorder, is no longer tenable. Furthermore, the treatment of GAD now includes both benzodiazepines and antidepressants, as with panic disorder (Nutt and Bell 1997). The efficacy of high-dose benzodiazepines in panic disorder would support the theory that

A Excessive anxiety and worry (apprehensive expectation), occurring more days than not for at least 6 months, about a number of events or activities (such as work or school performance).

B The person finds it difficult to control the worry.

C The anxiety and worry are associated with three (or more) of the following six symptoms (with at least some symptoms present for more days than not for the past 6 months). **Note:** only one item is required in children.

1   Restlessness or feeling keyed up or on edge
2   Being easily fatigued
3   Difficulty concentrating or mind going blank
4   Irritability
5   Muscle tension
6   Sleep disturbance (difficulty falling or staying asleep, or restless unsatisfying sleep)

D The focus of the anxiety and worry is not confined to features of an axis I disorder, e.g. the anxiety or worry is not about having a panic attack (as in panic disorder), being contaminated (as in obsessive–compulsive disorder), being away from home or close family relatives (as in separation anxiety disorder), gaining weight (as in anorexia nervosa), having multiple physical complaints (as in somatization disorder) or having a serious illness (as in hypochondriasis), and the anxiety and worry do not occur exclusively during post-traumatic stress disorder.

E The anxiety, worry or physical symptoms cause clinically significant distress or impairment in social, occupational or other important areas of functioning.

F The disturbance is not the result of the direct physiological effects of a substance (e.g. a drug of abuse, a medication) or a general medical condition (e.g. hyperthyroidism) and does not occur exclusively during a mood disorder, a psychotic disorder or a pervasive developmental disorder.

Table 10
Diagnostic criteria for generalized anxiety disorder

panic disorder differs from GAD only in the severity of the anxiety that is evident.

Klein has admitted that much of his work was on patients who had panic disorder and agoraphobia rather than panic disorder alone (Tyrer 1984). This may have been because only the most impaired were referred to specialist services. Thus, it is difficult from his data to extrapolate to those who have panic disorder without agoraphobia.

Perhaps the most compelling evidence of the separate nature of panic disorder and GAD comes from family aggregation studies. These show that panic disorder has a quite different pattern to GAD (Lepine and Pelissolo 1999).

Does panic disorder exist?

The fundamental features of the panic attacks seen in panic disorder were first described by Freud (Freud 1953):

1   They were sudden and unpredictable (lacking identifiable precipitants)

2   There was a fear of dying or losing control

3   The anxiety has associated somatic symptoms.

However, there is evidence that panic disorders are neither sudden nor unprovoked. The DSM-IV criterion for abrupt onset and rapid crescendo of panic (<10 minutes) has also been questioned in the light of a recent study (Scupi et al 1997). This compared panic disorder patients with rapid-onset panic in patients who fulfilled the other criteria but displayed prolonged onset panic. No significant difference in symptoms, course or comorbidity was found between the two groups.

Klein has suggested that the very unprovoked nature of the panic attacks of panic disorder is fundamental to the biological nature of its aetiology. Margraf et al (1987) recorded the heart rate of panic disorder patients during a period when they recorded in a diary all their panic attacks and the presence or absence of precipitants for those attacks. Interestingly, some of the attacks that were recorded as spontaneous actually occurred during periods of objective stress.

Panic attacks have a unique symptom complex and are difficult to confuse with any other psychiatric phenomena. Unfortunately panic attacks are not unique to panic disorder. The reliability of the diagnosis of panic attacks is therefore high, although the reliability of panic disorder itself is markedly less. It has been suggested that this is the result of problems with establishing the context of the panic attacks and whether they fit another diagnosis better.

Panic disorder and alcohol dependence

The relationship between alcohol dependence and anxiety states is a complex one. Many patients suggest that their anxiety state precedes their excessive alcohol consumption and is in fact an attempt to self-medicate (the tension-reduction theory of alcohol dependence). Alternatively, anxiety symptoms, including panic attacks, can be a direct result of withdrawal from alcohol. Thus, when interpreting the comorbidity of panic disorder and alcohol dependence, it is important to distinguish between withdrawal phenomena and independent anxiety symptoms. Schuckit and Hesselbrock (1994) have reviewed 10 studies of panic disorder among alcohol-dependent patients and found that, although rates of panic disorder were quoted as high as 60%, when the figures were adjusted to take into consideration symptoms caused by withdrawal and other substances (stimulants) the rates were much reduced (between 2% and 17%).

Similarly they showed that the mean adjusted rate of ago-raphobia in those with alcohol dependence was 9%. Another explanation for the association between alcohol dependence and panic disorder is that, through the process of repeated withdrawal, there may be perturbations of the noradrenaline (norepinephrine) and GABA (γ-aminobutyric acid) systems that cause panic symptoms (the kindling theory).

The evidence for an increased rate of alcohol dependence among those with panic disorder is somewhat inconclusive.

Onset

The mean age of onset of panic disorder is around 25 years. However, there appears to be a bimodal distribution (see page 16). It is of note that a significant proportion of people with panic disorder (7–11%) have their first panic attack very early in life, even before the age of 10 (Pollack and Smoller 1995, Faravelli and Paionni 1999).

Quality of life and associated disability *(Table 11)*

In recent years, the functional impairment of patients with panic disorder has acquired some prominence in the diagnosis of the condition, alongside the frequency of panic attacks and the presence of agoraphobia (Fyer et al 1996). The experience of depression also indicated that quality of life is very important when the efficacy and optimal length of various treatments are discussed. Furthermore, health services and health-care organizations are constantly under pressure to balance the need for provision of treatment with restricted resources and cost considerations. Therefore, understanding the extent to which panic disorder affects patients' lives as a whole is a key issue when it comes to planning for appropriate services.

Less time spent on hobbies

Increased marital dissatisfaction

Financial dependency

Subjective poor physical/emotional health

Increased health vistis

Increased risk of suicide

Alcohol and drug abuse

Extensive use of psychotropics

Table 11
Negative consequences of panic disorder

These questions have been addressed in large epidemiological studies. The Epidemiological Catchment Area (ECA) study used a sample from five communities in the USA, which included both treated and untreated patients. It was, therefore, more representative than a usual clinical sample, which may be biased towards the more severe end of the spectrum of the disorder, or lacking in severely agoraphobic patients who never receive treatment. Patients with a lifetime diagnosis of panic disorder and/or agoraphobia were compared with depressed patients (a condition with well-established detrimental effects on patients' overall function) and attendees who had other psychiatric conditions or were free of mental disorders. Panic disorder patients were found to experience severe social and health consequences. These consequences were comparable in severity and sometimes bigger than those seen in depressed patients. Social and marital functions were significantly impaired, and panic disorder was associated with financial dependency. Panic disorder patients subjectively experienced poor physical and emotional health. There was an increased risk of suicide, alcohol and drug abuse, as well as use of psychotropic medication (such as tranquillizers) (Markowitz et al 1989) (Table 11). The disability associated with panic disorder was found to be even higher in older or less educated patients, or when major depression was also present (Hollifield et al 1997).

Other community samples produced a similar picture. Panic disorder patients appear to be more severely impaired than patients with other anxiety disorders. Disability in relation to work is also extensive. Panic disorder patients are more likely to be unemployed or to earn less than 'normal' people who do the same jobs. The rate of those who are dependent on welfare or disability benefits exceeds 25% in some studies (Katerndahl and Realini 1997). Samples from primary care settings have also shown that panic disorder patients are more disabled (with more time lost from work and increased number of health visits) than controls with no mental disorders. This was even more pronounced when a comorbid condition was also present (Olfson et al 1997)

Health costs

In community studies, both panic and depressed patients were found to use more medical and psychiatric services than control populations, although panic disorder patients also showed a greater tendency to use hospital A&E departments (Markowitz et al 1989). The same picture emerged from a primary care sample (Roy-Byrne et al 1999). Panic disorder patients made more use of the

A&E, and medical and mental health visits, compared with a control group of psychiatrically healthy patients from the same practices.

An important aspect of the increased use of medical services is that a large number of patients do not receive appropriate treatment because they do not get a proper diagnosis and are diverted to the wrong clinics. In one study, 59% of patients attending a cardiology clinic with atypical chest pain were found to suffer from undiagnosed panic disorder (Beitman et al 1987).

The importance of the economic costs of anxiety disorders extends far beyond the direct treatment costs. When anxiety disorders were considered as a whole, their estimated cost in one calendar year (1990) in the USA was a staggering $US 46.6 billion, accounting for about 30% of the total expenditure for mental illness in that country. Furthermore, less than a quarter of this expenditure was for direct medical treatment; the remainder went on lost or reduced productivity (DuPont et al 1996). Although there was no breakdown of cost by specific anxiety diagnosis, it is safe to assume that panic disorder was responsible for a substantial chunk of this expenditure. Finally, a prospective study showed that, in a group of panic disorder patients, the direct annual health costs almost doubled during the year that followed the diagnosis, although the indirect costs of lost productivity during the same period decreased to one fifth of the year before (Salvador-Carulla et al 1995) (Figure 2).

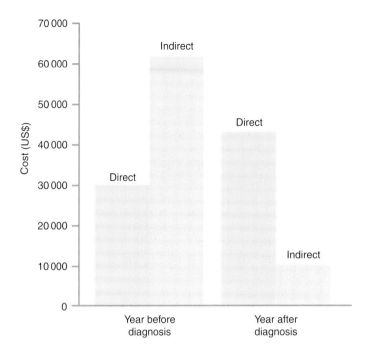

Figure 2
Annual direct and indirect health costs for a group of 61 panic patients (in US$). (From Salvador-Carulla et al 1995.)

The importance of subthreshold symptoms of panic disorder

Recent epidemiological studies have shown that there is a high prevalence of patients with subthreshold panic disorder symptoms in the community. These patients narrowly miss the criteria for diagnosis of the condition. In one study, subjects characterized as having infrequent panic attacks (at least one attack in the 6 months before their assessment) were compared with normal controls and panic disorder patients, on a series of measures of disability and health utilization. These patients were found to be almost as disabled in vocational, familial and social functioning as patients with full panic disorder, and significantly more so than the controls (Katon et al 1995). This finding comes, perhaps, as no surprise, because similar findings have been reported for depression and mixed anxiety–depression populations (Wells et al 1989, Broadhead et al 1990). Although some studies show the full syndrome to have a greater effect on the person with the condition than infrequent panic attacks, those with infrequent panic attacks are still significantly more disabled than normal controls (Katerndahl and Realini 1997).

It is argued that, because the prevalence of patients with infrequent panic attacks in the general population is higher than panic disorder itself, infrequent panic is likely to confer a higher risk of reduction of social and work function attributable to a population than panic disorder itself. The importance of such subthreshold morbidity in treatment and outcome has become the focus of systematic attention only recently. The concept of the panic–agoraphobic spectrum, which entails careful assessment and treatment of subtle symptoms, is gathering some empirical validation (Cassano et al 1997).

Lifetime course and outcome

Panic disorder is generally considered to be a chronic condition, and this is true when the main symptoms are studied. Although most patients improve, few seem to achieve full remission (Pollack et al 1990, Keller et al 1994, Roy-Byrne and Cowley 1994/95, Pollack and Otto 1997). It has been suggested, however, that this is an oversimplification of the course of panic, arising from methodological shortcomings of the follow-up studies (Katschnig and Amering 1998). Patient selection bias has been blamed for producing a worse overall outcome than in real life (Shinoda et al 1999). This is explained by the fact that patients with a quick recovery would stop attending follow-up sessions, so that subjects remaining in these studies represent more severely ill patients than the general population of patients with panic disorder. It has been pointed out, for example, that in epidemiological samples only a third of the cases have agoraphobia, whereas in clinical samples this rises to two-thirds (Katschnig and Amering 1998). The presence or absence of agoraphobia has a detrimental effect on the outcome of the condition, as discussed later.

In a prospective study, 423 patients were followed up 4 years after completing a pharmacological treatment trial (Katschnig et al 1996). A sizeable proportion (three out of five) was still experiencing occasional panic attacks and a significant number (two out of five) had at least moderate agoraphobia. However, the disability attributed to the illness had a more favourable outcome. About one in five patients was reporting dysfunction at work or home, whereas one in three still experienced difficulties in his or her social life. It should be noted that these patients experiencing symptoms did not necessarily fulfil the criteria for diagnosis of panic disorder at follow-up. The overall estimate arising from this prospective treatment study was that 31% of the patients remained in full remission after 4 years, 24% had an episodic course and 45% were persistently unwell (Figure 3) (Katschnig et al 1995). A worse outcome was seen in a study of a relatively treatment-resistant group of patients, who were followed up for up to 5 years. Most of the cases had improved and did not fulfil the diagnostic criteria for panic disorder when reassessed, but only 10% were found to be completely asymptomatic (Cowley et al 1996). Therefore, it appears that the outcome of panic disorder may be good in most cases, but a substantial proportion has a chronic condition and this should be taken into account when long-term treatment is considered.

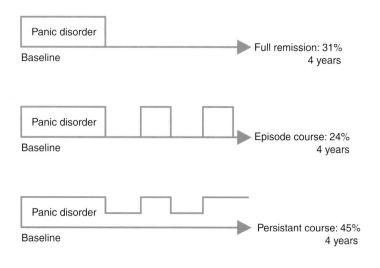

Figure 3
Outcome of panic disorder after 4-year follow up.
(From Katschnig et al 1995.)

What determines the course? *(Table 12)*

It is obvious from the previous section what the definition of 'full remission' is. The criteria for recovery in panic disorder should account not only for panic attacks, but also for ago-raphobia and social functioning. A study in Japan looked at the interplay of clinical and social factors in determining the outcome of panic disorder in a cohort of 65 outpatients who were treated with medication and brief psychotherapy, and were followed up for 1 year (Shinoda et al 1999). They showed that the presence of hypochondriasis at intake predicted the severity of clinical symptoms (panic attacks and agoraphobia) at the end of the study. The social function outcome was affected by the duration of the illness before the onset of treatment and the severity of the agoraphobia. Furthermore, the older the patients at the time of the onset of their illness, and the more severe their panic attacks, the more they improved socially during their year of treatment.

Female sex

Duration of illness

Comorbid depression/alcohol

Severity of agoraphobia

Hypochondriasis

Personality disorder

Interpersonal sensitivity

Medication side-effects

Failure to improve with treatment

Table 12
Predictors of poor outcome of panic disorder

A similar profile emerges from other studies as well (Katschnig et al 1996). Generally, agoraphobia and longer duration of illness at baseline, but not frequency of panic attacks, predict negative symptomatic outcome. The only consistent predictor of long-term disability in a specific area (work, family, social) is the extent of the baseline disability in the same life domain. The authors also raised the possibility of the existence of various panic disorder subtypes that may have a differential course and outcome.

The course and outcome of panic disorder are also influenced by the sex of the patient. Women are more likely to have panic attacks with agoraphobia, whereas men are more likely to have uncomplicated panic disorder. Women are also twice as likely to have recurrence of the disorder, after remission (Yonkers et al 1998). Other studies have indicated that personality disorder, interpersonal sensitivity, comorbid depression, alcohol and substance abuse, medication side effects and clinical status on discharge also influence the outcome negatively, although these factors are not universally accepted. The influence of life events on the outcome of panic has not been systematically studied. It is also questionable whether earlier onset, or the presence of anxiety symptoms and/or disorders in childhood, has a negative effect on the outcome of treatment, despite the fact that these patients appear to be more severely ill at baseline (Cowley et al 1996, Pollack et al 1996, Katschnig and Amering 1998).

Effect of treatment on the course of panic disorder

Treatment and contact with psychiatrists and/or psychologists do not seem to have a favourable effect on the outcome of panic disorder (Katschnig et al 1996). However, naturalistic studies such as the one mentioned above do not account for the differences in the quality of treatment. Specifically designed studies are needed to assess the true impact of the various forms of treatment on the long-term outcome of the disorder. When treatment regimens are scrutinized in primary care settings, they are often found to be suboptimal or insufficient (Roy-Byrne et al 1999). In this primary care naturalistic study, only 22% of the patients received adequate pharmacological treatment (type and/or dose of medication) and even fewer (12%) received adequate psychotherapy (defined as cognitive–behavioural therapy – CBT).

Ever since Klein suggested that panic disorder was a separate diagnostic entity on the basis of its specific response to imipramine, its aetiology has been the subject of much research. A bewildering diversity of factors has been implicated in its aetiology. Psychological theories, genetic and environmental contributions, challenge paradigms, imaging studies and the therapeutic benefit of certain drugs are just some of the numerous leads, that have proved difficult to assimilate into a meaningful unifying theory. In this chapter, we briefly summarize the available evidence and attempt, using the model suggested by Gorman et al (2000), to draw it together.

Cognitive theories

Clark (1998) proposed a model in which misinterpretations of symptoms are central to the cycle that produces panic. As depicted in Figure 4, a perceived threat causes apprehension and consequent bodily sensations, which are then misinterpreted in such a way as to exacerbate the apprehension and increase the intensity of the bodily sensations. The cycle ultimately leads to a panic attack. One possible explanation of why only some people go on to develop panic disorder after their first panic attack may be that, for the syndrome to take hold, the individual must have a certain cognitive set. Thus, if they have a tendency to ruminate on the initial panic experience, they become more vigilant about their own bodily sensations and are therefore more at risk of responding in a pathological fashion to the next experience of similar bodily sensations. They may also avoid precipitants that have already been identified as provoking the feared sensations. This avoidance serves to maintain the problem because patients incorrectly assume that, by this behaviour, they have averted some catastrophe. Challenging such avoidance is a central part of the treatment of panic disorder using this model.

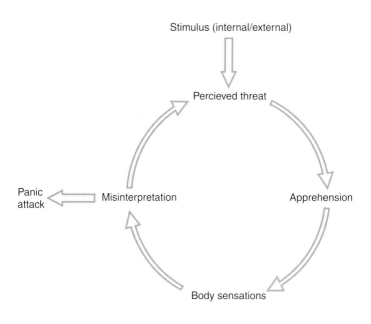

Figure 4
Clark's cognitive model of panic.

One of the most attractive features of Clark's work is that he has generated some predictions from his model that can be tested. These are as follows.

1   People who have panic disorder are more likely than those who don't to misinterpret bodily sensations catastrophically.

2   Such catastrophic misinterpretations in panic disorder patients serve to increase anxiety and panic.

3   Panic attacks triggered by challenges can be averted if the catastrophic misinterpretations are reduced or prevented.

4   Cognitive change is necessary to maintain treatment gains, even with drug treatment.

Psychodynamic theories

Shear and her colleagues (1993) performed video-taped psychodynamic interviews with nine patients who had a combination of panic disorder and agoraphobia. They identified a number of themes that included childhood anxiety and shyness, unsupportive parenting styles, and chronic feelings of being trapped and frustrated. They hypothesized that, in such panic disorder patients, there was an incomplete resolution of the conflict between dependence and independence, and that this was the result of an inherent fear of unfamiliar situations being exacerbated by controlling parenting styles in early life. From these themes they have proposed a psychodynamic model (Figure 5) which incorporates the concept of an inherent vulnerability to separation or suffocation and also a learned sense of inability to control panic (Klein 1993, Barlow 1998).

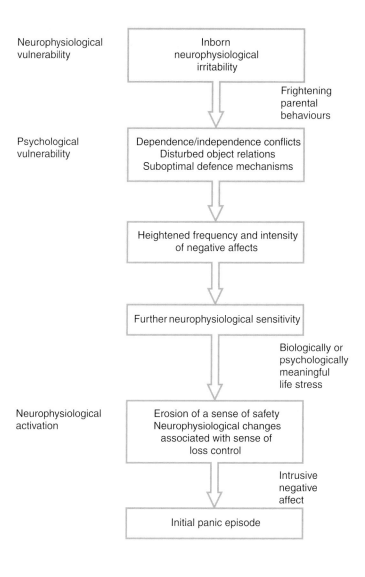

Figure 5
Psychodynamic model of panic disorder. (After Shear et al 1993.)

This model suggests that the biological tendency towards fearfulness is exacerbated by critical and controlling parenting, which in turn undermines progress to independence. The resulting fear of abandonment or being trapped causes increased anxiety. In the context of an inherently anxious person, this anxiety starts a vicious cycle, which culminates in a panic attack. This model proposes that panic attacks are triggered by thoughts, rather than being spontaneous as suggested by the neurobiological model. The model also stresses the possibility that unconscious and conscious fantasies of being trapped or abandoned may have a role in triggering panic.

Conditioning

It has been suggested that the trigger for panic can be explained using classic conditioning. In this model, hyperventilation acts as an unconditioned stimulus (UCS) that triggers anxiety and panic (an unconditioned response or UCR). Palpitations, which can occur at the same time as hyperventilation, may not initially arouse anxiety. However, through their association with hyperventilation (UCS) and the process of conditioning, palpitations may become a conditioned stimulus (CS), i.e. palpitations become capable of triggering panic (a conditioned response or CR) independently of hyperventilation.

The conditioning theory of the aetiology of panic disorder does not explain why panic disorder does not display extinction in studies where repeated arousals are not followed by panic attacks. Nor does it explain why fear is more easily conditioned to animals than to inanimate objects. Seligman (1988) proposed his evolutionary preparedness theory regarding such differences in the tendency to condition to certain stimuli. This proposed that certain stimuli, which posed a more fundamental threat to survival, had a greater potential for conditioning (e.g. heights, snakes or palpitations). He extrapolated that the coincidence of such stimuli (e.g. palpitations) with panic attack might be powerful enough to cause conditioning in a single exposure, which was difficult to extinguish. However this still does not explain why one person will go on to develop panic disorder after experiencing panic and palpitations whereas another does not.

Wolpe and Rowan (1988) make a distinction between the first panic attack that they attribute to independent psychological or biological precipitants and subsequent attacks, which they suggest are the result of classic conditioning. This is supported by clinical data showing that 92% of panic disorder patients in one study experienced their first panic attack in an anxiety-provoking situation rather than at home (Lelliot et al 1989). They also proposed a modification of classic conditioning as an explanation for the development of panic disorder. In this interoceptive model, they proposed that panic is caused by an abnormal conditioned response to physical sensations. Fundamental to this model is that anxiety provokes hyperventilation, which in turn causes dizziness and paraesthesia. After repeated experiences of anxiety, hyperventilation and its associated symptoms, these associated symptoms become conditioned stimuli and can provoke panic attacks in their own right. They concede that certain situations where escape is difficult (e.g. aeroplanes and buses) can also precipitate panic attacks. This model interprets catastrophic misinterpretation of these physical symptoms as a cognitive response to these unpleasant experiences and as an attempt to make sense of these sensations (Figure 6).

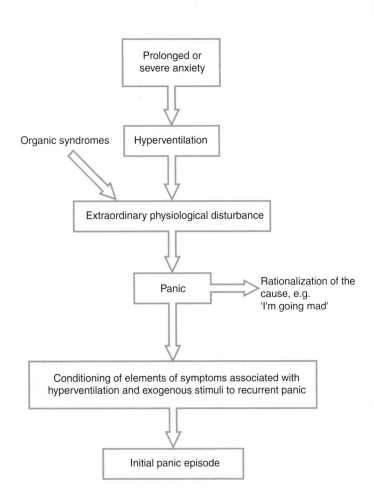

Figure 6
The development of panic disorder. (After Wolpe and Rowan 1988.)

A slightly different interpretation of such catastrophizing is provided by the anxiety sensitivity theory (McNally and Lorenz 1987). This states that, although the individual may well misinterpret bodily sensations, it is not this misinterpretation that drives the panic; rather it is the erroneous belief that the sensations themselves are inherently dangerous. Such a theory also differs from the interoceptive model because it does not require a process of development of abnormal conditioned responses to physical sensations. Critics have suggested that it represents little more than trait anxiety. It will now be evident that these different models share much in common. Similar concepts are described in different terms.

Genetic factors

Family studies

The aggregation of a disorder in families is suggestive, but not conclusive, of a genetic component in its aetiology. The lack of aggregation is, however, good evidence that there is no genetic component to the aetiology. In the six direct-interview studies of the families of panic disorder patients, the lifetime prevalence of panic disorder in relatives of a proband varied between 7.9% and 41%. The prevalence in families of controls varied between 0.8% and 8%, thus suggesting a possible genetic component to aetiology (Lepine and Pelissolo 1999).

Twin studies

The results from twin studies are somewhat mixed. The Virginia Twin Registry study (Kendler et al 1993) identified 63 pairs of twins with panic disorder. When the DSM-III-R criteria were applied, the concordance for monozygotes was 24% and for dizygotes only 11%. The heritability values were much less if fewer stringent diagnostic criteria were applied to this cohort. However, when the DSM-III criteria were applied to the Norwegian Twin Registry Study (Torgersen 1983) there was no significant difference in concordance between the two groups (one in five of the monozygotes and none of six of the dizygotes). A similar lack of difference between the monozygotes and dizygotes was seen in an Australian study (Andrews et al 1990). Thus, in individuals with identical genetic material the concordance rates are relatively low. This would suggest that, although some of the risk of developing panic disorder is heritable, not all of it is. Environmental factors are also an important role in triggering this panic disorder in individuals with a genetically predetermined diathesis (Fyer 2000).

Linkage studies

Linkage studies have attempted to identify which portion of the chromosome is responsible for the heritability of panic disorder. These have so far proved fruitless. Both methodical screens of the genome and the candidate gene approach have been used. The candidates that have so far shown no linkage include: α-haptoglobulin, the adrenergic receptors and several subunits of the GABA receptor system.

Childhood social factors

As has already been seen even in individuals with identical genetic material, the concordance rates are relatively low. This suggests that a vulnerability to develop panic disorder is inherited and that environmental factors are also important in triggering this condition.

The team at Duke University that participated in the ECA study investigated the relationship between panic disorder and a number of childhood traumas (Tweed et al 1989). They found that there was an association between separation from a parent during childhood and the later development of panic disorder and agoraphobia. A number of explanations for this are possible:

1 There is a causal link between early separation and panic disorder and agoraphobia

2 Parental separation was in fact a marker of another risk factor (e.g. an anxiety disorder in a parent)

3 The aftermath of the parental separation was in some way responsible.

In a study of adult panic disorder patients, Stein et al (1996) found that, in comparison to controls, the panic disorder patients reported significantly higher rates of sexual and physical abuse as children. The effect on emotional attachments at a formative age could predispose to later development of panic disorder by engendering fear. On a more biological level, Nemeroff (2000) has recently shown that abuse in infancy can be linked experimentally with alterations in the stress response in adulthood.

Others have speculated that separation anxiety in childhood was related to adult panic disorder. The results of retrospective surveys of the presence of childhood separation anxiety are mixed.

Parenting styles have been investigated using the Parenting Bond Instrument (PBI) (Parker et al 1975). This is a questionnaire designed to measure two dimensions of parenting: care and protection. In a comparison of panic disorder patients and normal controls, Faravelli et al (1991) found that the former scored their parents as significantly less caring and more controlling than the controls (Table 13). Parker (1979), also using the PBI, compared patients who had agoraphobia with patients who had social phobia. He found that those with agoraphobia recorded lower maternal care than those with social phobia. He noted that both groups recorded that their mothers had been over-protective. This would be consistent with Shear's (1993) hypothesis (discussed above) that a biological predis-position to anxiety is exacerbated by frightening parental behaviours. One possible problem with such studies is that they rely on the recollection of parenting styles in childhood by adults. Panic disorder patients may recollect their child-hood experiences in an excessively negative fashion because, in their adult life, they have come to attribute their problems to their upbringing.

Parental separation

Critical/overprotective parenting

Separation anxiety

Sexual abuse

Physical abuse

Table 13
Childhood risk factors for the development of panic disorder

Challenge studies *(Table 14)*

Lactate

Pitts and McClure discovered that lactate infusions can pre-cipitate panic attacks (Pitts and McClure 1967). A lactate challenge usually consists of the intravenous administration of 0.5mol/l of sodium lactate over 20 min. Lactate provokes anxiety in 85% of panic disorder patients and 25% of con-trols (Balon et al 1988). The anxiety induced in this way can be reduced by benzodiazepines, clonidine (which reduces noradrenaline function) and antidepressants such as imipramine. Reschke and his colleagues (1995) compared the prevalence of panic attacks in the relatives of panic disorder patients who were either sensitive or insensitive to a lactate challenge. They found that there was no difference in prevalence between the two groups. This would support the hypothesis that response to a lactate challenge is a state rather than a trait marker. Lactate also provokes anxiety in patients who have post-traumatic stress disorder but not in those with social phobia.

Transmitter	Panic promoting	Panic reducing
GABA	Flumazenil FG7142	High-potency benzodiazepines
Serotonin (5-HT)	*m*-Chlorophenylpiperazine (mCPP) Tryptophan depletion (in treated PD)	SSRIs or TCAs (chronically) Tryptophan (5-HT) 5-HTP
Noradrenaline	Yohimbine Isoproterenol ⎱ Action may not be specific to PD	
PD, panic disorder	TCAs, tricyclic antidepressants;	SSRIs, selective serotonin reuptake Inhibitors.

Table 14
Neurotransmitter systems implicated in the aetiology of panic disorder

There has been much speculation as to the panicogenic mechanism of lactate. A study of non-human primates appears to support the theory that the mechanism is a peripheral one because cerebrospinal fluid (CSF) measurements of lactate and carbon dioxide showed no change during lactate challenge (Coplan et al 1992). Possible peripheral mechanisms could include catastrophic misinterpretation of somatic symptoms triggered by lactate or a direct effect of lactate on the cardiovascular system. In contrast to these results, Dager et al (1995) have shown, using magnetic resonance spectroscopy, disproportionate rises of cerebral lactate concentrations in panic disorder patients during hyperventilation, in comparison to healthy controls.

Carbon dioxide

Inhalation of a single breath of 35% carbon dioxide provokes panic attacks in 70% of panic disorder patients and 10% of controls. This is not the case in obsessive–compulsive disorder. The vulnerability of panic disorder patients to panic attacks provoked by carbon dioxide is diminished by successful treatment with clonazepam or fluvoxamine (Malizia and Nutt 1999).

Cholecystokinin-4

Cholecystokinin-4 (CCK-4) is capable of provoking both panic attacks in panic disorder patients and anxiety symptoms in normal controls. CCK-4 induces similar respiratory symptoms to inhalation of 35% carbon dioxide. It also acts as a respiratory stimulant in normal controls. The CCK-4 antagonist, L-365,250, has been shown to alleviate panic symptoms precipitated by CCK-4, but unfortunately it proved less effective in naturally occurring panic disorder itself (Bradwejn et al 1994).

Respiratory control as a common pathway in the aetiology of panic disorder

As noted above, lactate, carbon dioxide and CCK-4 all have the ability to provoke panic attacks and have been implicated in alterations in respiratory control. Klein (1993) hypothesized that panic disorder was the result of an abnormally sensitive suffocation alarm in the brain stem. Thus, in vulnerable individuals, activation of this alarm system provokes hyperventilation with associated fear and attempts to flee. Support for this theory comes from studies on children with a congenital hypoventilatory syndrome. These children lack the normal automatic drive to breathe, presumably because they lack the suffocation monitor. In a study of 13 such children, Pine et al (1994) showed that they had the lowest incidence of anxiety disorders. Interestingly they also compared them with children with asthma and found that the children with asthma had the highest rates of anxiety disorder. As already noted earlier (page 14) there is an increased incidence of panic disorder in those who have respiratory disease. Taken together, these clinical abnormalities suggest a significant role for respiratory factors in panic disorder.

Klein's false suffocation alarm theory bears some striking similarities to Barlow's (1998) description of spontaneous panic attacks as false alarms. Barlow proposed that true alarms occurred in the event of actual external threat and learned alarms were conditioned panic attacks.

Neurochemistry

The evidence regarding the involvement of neurotransmitters in the aetiology of panic disorder can best be described as circumstantial and is based on speculation about the efficacy of certain drugs as treatments of panic disorder. The strongest evidence available on these grounds is for the involvement of GABA and serotonin (5-HT). There is less evidence for noradrenaline and very little to suggest a role for dopamine in panic disorder.

GABA

The high-potency benzodiazepines (alprazolam and clonazepam) show efficacy in controlling panic attacks. These drugs bind to the benzodiazepine receptor (part of the GABA-receptor complex) and allosterically promote the action of GABA. Endogenous GABA binds to this complex and promotes membrane hyperpolarization by widening the chloride channel at the centre of the receptor complex. Under normal circumstances, the benzodiazepine antagonist flumazenil has no direct effect on GABA function and the inverse agonists (e.g. FG 7142) decrease the effects of GABA. However, in panic disorder patients, there is evidence that flumazenil is panicogenic and that the benzodiazepines have reduced efficacy. It has been suggested that this is a result of a shift in the GABA–benzodiazepine spectrum of activity (Figure 7). One explanation for this phenomenon is that, in panic disorder, there is a compensatory release of endogenous GABA–benzodiazepine agonist in an attempt to reduce the anxiety symptoms. Therefore, with the addition of flumazenil, this agonist is displaced and there are rebound panic symptoms (Nutt et al 1990).

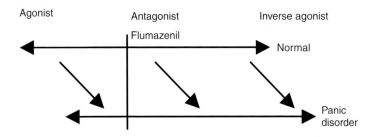

Figure 7
Panicogenic effect of flumazenil.

Serotonin

Both selective serotonin reuptake inhibitors and tricyclic antidepressant drugs (e.g. clomipramine) acutely exacerbate panic symptoms, although in the long term they alleviate them. This finding has been explained by two hypotheses with regard to serotonin. The first, the serotonin excess theory, suggests that panic results from either excess levels of serotonin or excess postsynaptic sensitivity to serotonin. If this is the case, the acute exacerbation of anxiety seen with selective serotonin reuptake inhibitors (SSRIs) and tricyclic antidepressants may be caused by the initial rise in synaptic serotonin concentration, and the subsequent reduction in anxiety symptoms may be the result of gradual postsynaptic downregulation of these receptors with time.

The second, the serotonin deficit theory, holds that a specific regional serotonin deficit, namely in the periaqueductal grey area (PAG), is responsible for panic disorder. This theory proposes that serotonin in the PAG normally has an inhibitory role in panic behaviour. The initial exacerbation of anxiety symptoms by SSRIs may be caused by the increased levels of serotonin stimulating the presynaptic autoreceptors ($5\text{-}HT_{1A}$), consequently causing a transient overall fall in the synaptic serotonin concentration. The exacerbation of the panic symptoms wears off when the $5\text{-}HT_{1A}$ receptors become desensitized.

Neither serotonin nor its precursor tryptophan precipitate panic attacks; in fact, they both actually reduce levels of anxiety. Fenfluramine is an indirect serotonin agonist that provokes anxiety although not specifically panic attacks. The relatively non-selective $5\text{-}HT_2$ agonist *m*-chlorophenylpiperazine (mCPP) induces panic attacks in patients with panic disorder at low doses, but not in healthy controls (Table 14) (Bell and Nutt 1998).

Noradrenaline

Drugs acting solely to raise noradrenaline concentrations have not shown any efficacy in reducing panic attacks. The main noradrenaline nucleus, the locus ceruleus, is thought to be responsible for orientating and alerting activities. Thus, promotion of noradrenaline is thought to have non-specific action to heighten response to stimulation of all kinds, not just anxiety-related ones. The synaptic concentration of noradrenaline is governed in part by the presynaptic α_2-autoreceptor. Activation of this autoreceptor reduces the release of further noradrenaline into the synapse. Yohimbine is an α_2-receptor antagonist that raises the synaptic concentration of noradrenaline and precipitates panic attacks in 60% of those who have panic disorder and only 5% of control subjects. However, these panic attacks were slightly different phenomenologically from those occurring spontaneously and are not affected by fluvoxamine, which normally alleviates panic disorder (Goddard et al 1993) It may be that this promotion of panic attacks is caused by a non-specific action to precipitate a variety of anxiety presentations mediated by increased noradrenaline.

Isoproterenol is a non-selective β agonist that has been reported to precipitate panic attacks by Pohl et al (1988). One possibility is that panic attacks are precipitated by iso-proterenol because it induces palpitations, which are then misinterpreted by the patient.

Imaging and panic disorder

Measures of brain structure

In a magnetic resonance imaging (MRI) study, temporal lobe abnormalities were found in one-third of a sample of panic disorder patients (11 of 30) but only one of 20 controls (Ontiveros et al 1989). If the result of this study were to be replicated, it would be interesting to establish whether these structural differences were the cause of the disorder or a result of it.

Measures of brain receptors

Malizia et al (1997) undertook a positron emission tomography (PET) study using the $GABA_A$ benzodiazepine ligand [^{11}C] flumazenil, comparing panic disorder patients who were benzodiazepine naive with controls. They found that the panic disorder patients showed decreased [^{11}C] flumazenil binding in the inferior parietal temporo-occipital areas. This reduction in $GABA_A$ benzodiazepine-binding sites could be responsible for an increased tendency to suffer anxiety because it would represent a reduction in the overall brain inhibitory tone. These findings may suggest a possible causal role for GABA in the aetiology of panic disorder.

Identifying brain circuits

Other researchers have attempted to use ^{15}O-labelled water in PET studies to quantify regional blood flow during provoked panic attacks. Much of the research in this field has identified regional vasoconstriction during provoked panic attacks. However, hyperventilation is a common response to panicogens and this, in itself, causes regional vasoconstriction via reduced blood carbon dioxide. Gorman et al (2000) have reported preliminary results that suggest that, even when the degree of hypocapnia is controlled for, panic disorder patients display greater regional vasoconstriction than control when challenged with a panicogen. Furthermore, Doppler ultrasonography studies have shown that panic disorder patients show a greater reduction in basilar artery flow in response to hyperventilation (Gorman et al 2000).

A model of the aetiology of panic disorder

Gorman et al (2000) have proposed an attractive hypothesis, in the form of their neuroanatomical model, to incorporate the diverse evidence for the aetiology of panic disorder outlined above. Drawing from pre-clinical animal work with conditioned fear, a fear circuit has been suggested (Figure 8). The focus of this model, is the central nucleus of the amygdala, which serves as a relay station between the higher centres (sensory thalamus, prefrontal cortex and sensory motor cortex) and the brain-stem efferent nuclei. The flow of information in the higher centres is in both directions to and from the amygdala, and also between these higher centres themselves. This model therefore proposes that the amygdala receives not only afferent sensory information but also afferents from the higher centres representing cognitive processing of that information. Abnormalities in this cognitive processing could form the basis of the catastrophic thinking, detailed by Clark (1988), in his cognitive model of panic disorder. Other factors that could influence the response to perceived threat include a genetic predisposition to fearfulness exacerbated by over-critical/controlling parenting styles (Shear et al 1993). Preclinical experiments also implicate structures known to be part of the proposed fear network. In conditioned-fear experiments rats display contextual learning, which is dependent on an intact connection between the hippocampus and the amygdala. Thus, a rat trained to associate a tone with an electric shock will also learn to associate the cage in which the experiment was performed with the noxious stimulus. However, if the tract linking the hippocampus and amygdala is severed, the rat no longer displays fear when confronted by the cage, although it continues to do so with the tone. If the amygdala is lesioned, the rat responds to the cage but not to the tone (Kim and Fanselow 1992).

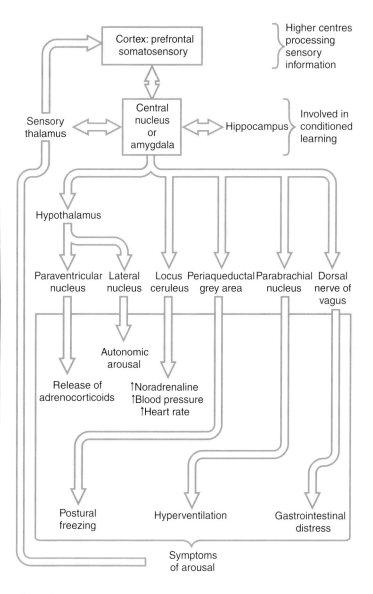

Figure 8

Neuroanatomical model of panic disorder. (Adapted from Gorman et al 2000.)

As can be seen from Figure 8 the symptoms triggered by each of the brain-stem nuclei are as familiar as the autonomic symptoms associated with panic. However, not all panic attacks are characterized by all these symptoms. It has been suggested that this indicates that these autonomic symptoms, rather than being causal in panic disorder, are in fact epiphenomenon. Gorman suggests that the central abnormality underlying panic disorder is an abnormally sensitive fear circuit. This sensitivity may be partly genetically predetermined and partly environmentally influenced (early life experiences). This theory thus accommodates the evidence already detailed above that a variety of challenges is capable of precipitating panic attacks. The postulated abnormally sensitive fear circuit responds to unsettling afferent sensory information, which would normally be tolerated, by setting in train the autonomic responses and also accompanying cognitions characteristic of panic disorder. The SSRIs may serve to damp down this autonomic arousal and benzodiazepines may modulate the impaired appraisal of threat, which leads to these characteristic cognitions (Middleton 1991) (Figure 9).

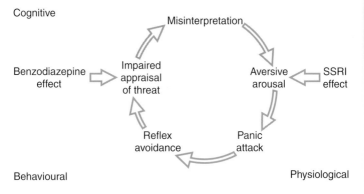

Figure 9
Proposed sites of action of SSRIs and benzodiazepines in relation to cognitive, physiological and behavioural components of panic disorder.
(After Middleton 1991.)

56

Conclusion

The understanding of the aetiology of panic disorder is developing in many diverse areas. Family studies suggest that there is a genetic predisposition to panic disorder. Early life experiences, such as parenting styles and parental separation, have also been implicated. Eloquent psychological models incorporating genetically determined neurophysiological differences in response to stress and the influence of formative relationships have been produced. Biological studies have shown that brain-stem structures trigger the familiar autonomic symptoms seen in panic attacks. It is proposed that panic disorder may represent an abnormal sensitivity to this sensory information with pathologically extreme responses, possibly as a result of a defective brain GABA-inhibitory system.

Depression and panic disorder

Extent and importance of depression and panic disorder comorbidity

Depression and panic disorder are both common psychiatric conditions. Traditionally, they have been seen as distinct entities. However, their extensive comorbidity casts doubt on the validity of this distinction. Comorbidity is defined as the presence of more than one disorder in a person over a lifetime, or in a certain period of time. It appears to be the norm rather than the exception in the case of anxiety disorders and depression (Wittchen 1996a).

The study of comorbidity may have important implications for nosology, but its significance extends beyond this theoretical point of view. The interface of anxiety and depression affects the course and treatment outcome of these conditions (see also chapters on course and treatment). Patients with coexisting panic and depressive disorders tend to have more severe symptoms and are more impaired in their psychosocial functioning. According to some reports, they show a slower and lower response to treatment and, overall, have poorer prognosis, compared with patients who have just one condition (Figure 10). Suicide and self-harm are more common in this group of patients than in patients with either syndrome alone (Gorman 1996/97, Roy-Byrne et al 2000). Autonomic arousal is increased in the mixed group, as indicated by higher diastolic and systolic blood pressures and higher cardiac load, compared with patients with only panic disorder or depression (Townsend et al 1998). Therefore, exploring the relationship between the two conditions may produce important insights into the aetiology, diagnosis, treatment and outcome.

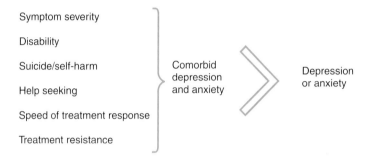

Symptom severity

Disability

Suicide/self-harm

Help seeking

Speed of treatment response

Treatment resistance

Comorbid depression and anxiety

Depression or anxiety

Figure 10
The relative importance of depression and panic comorbidity.

In general, comorbidity appears to be the rule among patients with depression, with about two-thirds having at least one comorbid anxiety disorder (Kessler et al 1996). In some studies, the estimate of depressive patients who have comorbid panic is as high as 37–54% (Gorman 1996/97). A bigger community sample, however, gave the more conservative estimate of 13% (Regier et al 1998). The percentage of panic disorder patients who experienced at least one depressive episode in their lifetime varies widely between studies, from 20% to 90%. An estimate of about 50% is what most experts accept (Gorman 1996/97). Overall, comorbid lifetime presentations are more frequent than pure ones (Angst et al 1997).

Symptom patterns of comorbidity

Panic disorder tends to predate depression rather than the other way round (Kessler et al 1996), although this is not a universal finding (Regier et al 1998). Symptoms of both disorders can be present during the same episode of illness. In this case, the patient may fulfil the diagnostic criteria for both conditions at the same time, or either of the two may present at a subthreshold level (Angst et al 1997). Subthreshold symptoms of panic disorder that may appear during a depressive episode include panic attacks, increased vasomotor responses, emotional lability, perceptual distortions, depersonalization and derealization. On the other hand, panic patients may experience persistent low mood, worsening of their symptoms in the morning, early morning wakening, suicidal ideation and psychomotor retardation (Hamilton 1983). Following a panic attack, mood is often very low for hours or days on end.

Models of depression and panic disorder comorbidity (Figure 11)

A number of models have been put forward in an attempt to explain the link between panic disorder and depression. The boundaries between the two conditions are described in the classification systems, but the presence of patients falling between these categories is undoubted (Angst 1997). The 'mixed' model postulates that the co-occurrence of depressive and anxiety symptoms delineates a separate category, a disorder in itself. For non-panic anxiety, this view is incorporated in ICD-10 and DSM-IV, with the introduction of mixed anxiety and depression as a separate diagnosis.

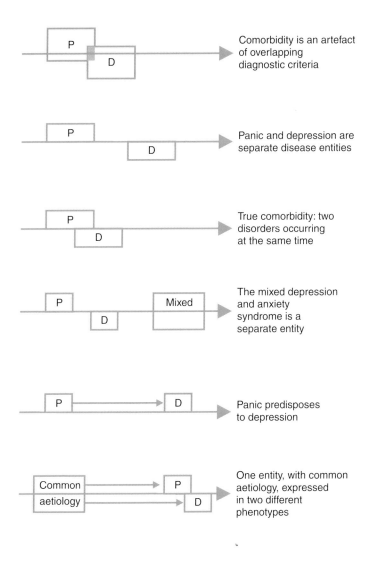

Figure 11
Models of comorbidity of depression and panic.
(After Wittchen 1996a; Stahl 1997; Frances et al 1992.)

Another model proposes that comorbidity is a chance finding, an artefact of the application of too many distinct anxiety and depressive disorders, which are very narrowly defined but have extensive definitional overlap. The modern classification also encourages multiple diagnosis, resulting in much increased rates of comorbidity in recent epidemiological studies. This idea seems implausible, because the rates of association of anxiety and depression are 20–30 times higher than what would have been expected if the disorders were independent (Kloss and Cameron 1992). It is therefore unlikely that the observed comorbidity of depression and panic can be explained purely by chance, or by the changes in our diagnostic habits (Frances et al 1992, Wittchen 1996a). The statistical association of depression and panic appears to endorse the clinical observation of the presence of depressive syndromes in patients with anxiety disorders, and vice versa.

A number of other models have also been put forward to explain comorbidity (Frances et al 1992, Stahl 1997). The 'separatist' model sees panic and depression as distinct conditions. The overlap is explained by the observation that both syndromes are common enough to be expected to co-occur by chance. For years, this model has been driving research into aetiological factors (both biological and psychological), separating various mental illnesses from one another. The 'comorbid' model is more atheoretical, and it accepts that two separate disorders may occur, in the same individual, at the same time, without necessarily being aetiologically linked.

The fact that panic appears to predate the development of depression lends support to the 'predispositional' model. Panic, or other forms of anxiety, could lead to depression through psychological or biological mechanisms, or both. This is illustrated in a process pathway proposed in Figure 12 (Wittchen 1996b).

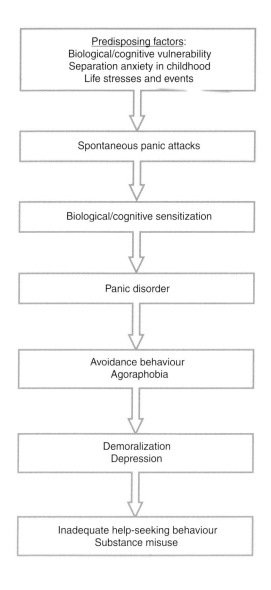

Figure 12
A pathway to panic and depression comorbidity. (From Wittchen 1996b).

It can be argued that, evoking the shared genetic and biological features of panic and depression and the treatment studies, the splitting of the conditions is artificial, and that a 'continuum' model is more attractive. This can also account for the fact that depression may predate panic, as well as appear later in life. Although patients with 'pure' syndromes undoubtedly exist, would it be preferable to include both mood and anxiety disorders in one diagnostic group? Finally, a 'combined' model accepts that all of the above hypotheses have some heuristic value in helping us to understand the relationship between panic anxiety and depression. Focusing on both the common factors and the differences between the syndromes should help the clarification of the aetiology, and lead to improvements in classification and treatment of this group of patients.

Biological and psychological overlap and the discrimination of depression and panic disorder

To what extent can shared and discriminating neurobiological and psychological mechanisms explain comorbidity of panic disorder and depression? A review of the biological overlap points at the genetic link between the two disorders (Gorman 1996/97). Relatives of patients with comorbid panic and depression are at a higher risk of developing mood, anxiety and alcohol abuse disorders, compared with relatives of patients who have depression alone. Relatives of patients with pure depression are also at higher risk of developing anxiety disorders, including panic disorder. These findings suggest a familial relationship between depression and anxiety in general, and panic disorder in particular, which requires further investigation. Depression and panic disorder share, to varying degrees, a number of neuroendocrinological abnormalities. These include blunted growth hormone response and hypothalamic–pituitary–adrenal (HPA) axis dysregulation. There is also evidence of disregulation of serotonin neurotransmission in both conditions. The neurobiology of panic disorder, with reference to these findings, is discussed earlier (see chapter on Causation and mechanisms).

However, there are also clear differences between panic disorder and depression. When present in the same patient, the results of challenge tests resemble those of pure panic disorder. e.g. intravenous lactate infusion and oral fenfluramine produce anxiety in panic disorder patients and in those with comorbid depression and panic disorder. On the other hand, they have almost no such effect in patients with pure depression (Gorman 1996/97). Furthermore, epidemiological data on the sex differences in depression support the hypothesis of a sex-specific subtyping of depression. It has been argued that pure depression has an equal sex ratio and is different from depression with comorbid panic disorder and anxiety, which is more prevalent in women. This finding may explain the overall higher prevalence of depression in women (Angst et al 1997, Silverstein 1999). Conversely, the higher prevalence of anxiety disorders in women has also been explained by comorbidity with depression (Carter et al 1999). Clearly, the elucidation of this complex sex comorbidity issue will help to clarify the nosological status of the mixed conditions.

As mentioned earlier, the comorbidity of panic disorder and depression predicts the severity of illness and treatment outcome. The treatment implications of comorbidity are discussed further in the next chapter.

Prevention

Until firm genetic or environmental predictors of later development of panic disorder are identified, not much can be
done by way of preventing the disorder. However, as discussed earlier, the outcome of panic disorder, especially
social functioning, is inversely correlated with the length of
illness before the onset of treatment (Shinoda et al 1999).
Therefore, an effective preventive strategy would aim to
reduce the time lag between the onset of the illness and ini-
tiation of treatment. For this to happen, the factors causing
this delay should be understood and addressed properly.
Lack of knowledge on the part of physicians about the
nature of panic disorder may delay the diagnosis and initi-
ation of appropriate treatment, and lead to extensive
unnecessary physical and laboratory investigations. The
general educational level of a society and the ways in which
its members relate with health services, as well as their
attribution of meaning to symptoms, may also affect their
seeking appropriate care.

The accessibility and availability of appropriate treatments
are also an important factor. Although education on mental
health issues can generally increase understanding and

speed up the search for care, help is sometimes not easily accessible. Services are expanding but the availability of specialist psychological treatments is not what it should be. Patients who have to wait for a long time before they are evaluated by a specialist may have their agoraphobia and avoidance more entrenched, thereby negatively affecting their clinical outcome.

Treatment

The last 20 years have seen an explosion in studies of the treatment of panic disorder. Drugs that have been available for some time, such as the tricyclic antidepressants and the benzodiazepines, have been successfully tested in randomized controlled trials. New compounds, such as the serotonin reuptake inhibitors, have also been found to be effective. In the meantime, psychological therapies have advanced, with the development of specific theoretical models that have proved their worth in subsequent treatment trials. In the rest of this chapter, we summarize the evidence for these treatment modalities and outline some of the problems and pitfalls in this area of research. Guidelines have also appeared in recent years, in an attempt to help the busy clinician make better decisions when he or she faces a patient with panic disorder and/or agoraphobia (American Psychiatric Association 1998, Ballenger et al 1998a). It should be remembered, however, that all such guidelines should be treated as provisional and subject to revisions, after new discoveries and refinements in treatment.

General measures

After the evaluation of symptoms and disability, and the diagnosis of panic disorder with or without agoraphobia, a series of general considerations and measures helps to ensure appropriate treatment and optimize outcome. As a norm, panic disorder patients are treated as outpatients.

The rare occasions on which they may require admission to inpatient settings are usually caused by pronounced suicidal ideation or the need for detoxification, when there is comorbid depression or substance abuse, respectively. Reassurance and education about the nature of the condition are crucial elements at the onset of any therapeutic intervention. This should extend, whenever appropriate, to the patient's family, or others who are expected to provide support or have to cope with the consequences of the illness. Contact with other specialists, especially those who are repeatedly asked to perform complex medical investigations to reassure the patient that there is no underlying physical condition, may be required. This includes A&E departments, where panic patients often present in 'medical' crisis. Good clinical management is dependent upon the establishment of a therapeutic relationship and treatment plan, careful evaluation and regular monitoring of progress, compliance, side effects or signs of worsening and lack of response (American Psychiatric Association 1998).

Pharmacological treatments

Selective serotonin reuptake inhibitors

Several double-blind, randomized trials (some of them large multicentre ones) have now demonstrated the efficacy of selective serotonin reuptake inhibitors (SSRIs) in the acute treatment of panic disorder. Most of the data available are for paroxetine, which was the first SSRI to be licensed for this indication. Studies of paroxetine included comparisons with placebo (Ballenger et al 1998b), clomipramine and placebo (Lecrubier et al 1997), or a combination of paroxetine and cognitive therapy versus the combination of placebo and cognitive therapy (Oehrberg et al 1995). In the first study, 86% of patients on 40 mg paroxetine responded versus 50% on placebo. In the second study, paroxetine (average dose 39 mg/day) was equally effective as clomipramine (average dose 92 mg/day), and both were significantly better than placebo. In the third study, the combination of active drug and psychotherapy brought about improvement in more patients (82%) than the combination of placebo and therapy (50%). A more recent 12-week study examined paroxetine versus clomipramine versus cognitive therapy (Bakker et al 1999). Again, the two medications were consistently superior to placebo, whereas cognitive therapy was better than placebo in some outcome measures.

Similar results to paroxetine are produced when other SSRIs are studied in a randomized fashion. Citalopram (Wade et al 1997), fluvoxamine (Hoehn-Saric et al 1993), fluoxetine (Michelson et al 1998) and sertraline (Londborg et al 1998, Pollack et al 1998) are all effective in treating panic disorder. Ballenger (1999) reviews the evidence for the SSRIs in panic disorder. All major symptoms appear to be responsive: panic attacks, agoraphobic symptoms and anticipatory anxiety between attacks; the quality of life also improves substantially. Furthermore, a meta-analysis of randomized SSRI studies suggests that the size of the effect for improvement with this class of drugs is greater than that with imipramine or alprazolam (Boyer 1995).

Long-term studies, up to 1 year, have also been published with paroxetine (Lecrubier and Judge 1997), citalopram (Lepola et al 1998) and fluoxetine (Michelson et al 1999) These studies show that the initial gains are maintained without any evidence for development of tolerance. If anything, there is evidence for continuing improvement, supporting the argument for long-term treatment of panic disorder.

The SSRIs are usually very well tolerated in panic (Table 15). In one long-term study comparing paroxetine with placebo and clomipramine, over 48 weeks of treatment fewer patients on paroxetine (7%) or placebo (9%) left the study because of side effects than with clomipramine (19%) (Lecrubier and Judge 1997). The SSRIs are safe in overdose, compared with tricyclic antidepressants, and they do not affect the cardiovascular function (see later). Common side effects include gastrointestinal disturbance, insomnia or drowsiness, sexual dysfunction, headaches, nocturnal sweating and, sometimes, increased anxiety. This may be particularly manifest at the onset of treatment, when patients experience an initial jitteriness, shakiness, agitation and increased frequency of panic attacks. This syndrome, also prominent with tricyclic antidepressants, may compromise compliance. Onset of treatment with low doses, e.g. 10 mg paroxetine (or comparable dose of another SSRI) for a week to 10 days, before escalation to a standard therapeutic dose, usually circumvents this problem (American Psychiatric Association 1998). An alternative strategy is to provide short-term cover with a high-potency benzodiazepine, e.g. clonazepam or alprazolam, for a couple of weeks. This initial worsening of anxiety is discussed in more detail in the section on tricyclic antidepressants.

The favourable side-effect profile of the SSRIs compared with the tricyclic antidepressants, and the lack of dependence and abuse potential compared with the benzodiazepines, established the SSRIs as the first-line option for pharmacological treatment of panic disorder. Furthermore, they have the advantage, over benzodiazepines, of treating any comorbid affective illness. The optimum dose of paroxetine in panic disorder, arising out of the studies mentioned earlier, is around 40 mg/day and for citalopram 20-30 mg/day. It is generally thought that panic disorder lies somewhere between depression and obsessive–compulsive disorder in terms of the SSRI dose needed to bring about significant clinical improvement. However, there have been large treatment studies where doses comparable to

	SSRIs (Selective serotonin reuptake inhibitors)	TCAs (Tricyclic antidepressants)	MAOIs (Monomine oxidase inhibitors)	BDZs (Benzodiazepines)
Onset of action	slow	slow	slow	fast
Initial exacerbation of anxiety	+/-	+/-	-	-
Therapeutic tolerance	-	-	-	little
Withdrawal	+	+	+	++
Abuse potential	-	-	-	+
Interactions with ethanol	+	+	++	+++
Dietary restrictions	-	-	+++	-
Sedation	-	++	-	++
Overdose risks	-	++	++	-

Table 15
Relative side effects of anti-panic drugs.

those used in depression were equally effective in panic disorder (Londborg et al 1998). Treatment should be continued for 12–24 months and then the medication should be tapered slowly over 4–6 months (Ballenger et al 1998a). So far, there have been no direct comparisons between the SSRIs in panic disorder, so the choice between them rests on appreciation of the strength of the available information, approval by regulatory authorities for the specific indication, the clinician's familiarity with the different compounds and the patient's previous response to these drugs.

There is characteristic SSRI discontinuation syndrome (Haddad 1998) and it is more pronounced with drugs with a shorter half-life. It is usually mild and starts within 2–3 days of stopping treatment (or longer in the case of fluoxetine), resolving spontaneously within 2–3 weeks. Reinstatement of the SSRI resolves the withdrawal symptoms. Common features are dizziness and vertigo, lightheadedness, nausea or vomiting, headaches, lethargy, anxiety and agitation or irritability, paraesthesiae, tremor, sweating, insomnia and diarrhoea. The prevalence of this syndrome is unknown as yet. Tapering of medication helps to minimize or avoid these symptoms.

Tricyclic antidepressants

The extrapolation of panic disorder from the old category of anxiety neurosis owes a lot to the original demonstration that imipramine was effective in treating those of the anxious patients who had panic attacks (Klein 1964). Since that first randomized, placebo-controlled trial, over 10 other randomized trials have consistently demonstrated the superiority of imipramine over placebo in the treatment of panic disorder (American Psychiatric Association 1998). Imipramine became the gold standard against which other potential pharmacological and psychological treatments of panic have been compared over the years.

The response rate (panic-free patients) with imipramine ranges from 45% to 70%, whereas that of placebo was found to be highly variable, between 15% and 50%. The improvement of panic disorder with imipramine, or other antidepressants, is not dependent on the treatment of concurrent affective illness. The dose is similar to that used for depression (100–150 mg/day), although not many proper dose-finding studies have been carried out, and it has been argued that panic disorder patients may respond to lower doses than depressed patients. The clinical response is, however, somewhat slower than depression. Substantial improvement is seen in the first 4–6 weeks, but the maximum effect may not be apparent until 10–12 weeks into treatment. Frequency and severity of panic attacks are the first symptoms to respond to imipramine. Reduction in anticipatory anxiety between the attacks follows the reduction in number and severity of the attacks. Improvement in avoidance and agoraphobia sometimes takes months before it becomes clinically significant (American Psychiatric Association 1998, Rosenberg 1999). Although this has been used as an argument against the use of medication in panic disorder, it is reasonable to expect this course of events. After patients experience a reduction in their panic attacks, they need some time of stability to digest their progress and reduce their anticipatory anxiety. A further period of consolidation is needed before they are ready gradually to confront the situations that trouble them the most.

The various tricyclic antidepressants have similar efficacy in depression, so one would expect the same in panic disorder. Few controlled trials have been performed with tricyclic antidepressants other than imipramine, however. In some studies, clomipramine has proved to be at least as effective as, if not more effective than, imipramine (Modigh et al 1992). However, trials with tricyclic antidepressants that act through noradrenaline rather than serotonin reuptake inhibition have not been as successful. A trial of desipramine showed only a trend of superiority over placebo, although the response for the latter group, at 76%, was exceptionally high (Lydiard et al 1993). Lofepramine was compared with clomipramine and placebo (Fahy et al 1992). At the end of the 24-week study period, 95% of the clomipramine patients were panic free, compared with 64% on lofepramine and 60% on placebo. Maprotiline, a tetracyclic noreadrenaline reuptake inhibitor, was found to be less effective than the SSRI fluvoxamine (Den Boer and Westenberg 1988).

The tricyclic antidepressants and related compounds have some well-documented side effects. These are anticholinergic (dry mouth, constipation, urinary hesitancy, blurred vision), cardiovascular (orthostatic hypotension, increased heart rate at rest), weight gain, nocturnal sweating, sexual dysfunction, drowsiness and fatigue. Therefore, they are not recommended for patients with cardiovascular problems or men with hypertrophy of the prostatic gland. Furthermore, they are dangerous in overdose, leading to death if they are ingested in high quantities.

An important clinical phenomenon that occurs in the early stages of treatment of panic, but not of pure depression, with tricyclic antidepressants is the paradoxical and transient increase in anxiety and number of panic attacks. Drugs with predominantly serotonergic action, such as clomipramine, are more likely to produce this syndrome, along with dizziness, anorexia and nausea. This is contrasted with the so-called 'jitteriness syndrome', which is an amphetamine-like stimulation produced by predominantly noradrenergic drugs, and characterized by agitation, insomnia, irritability and increased energy (Ramos et al 1993). The reality is that patients often experience symptoms from both sets, and they affect around 50% of the panic disorder patients treated with tricyclic antidepressants, although transiently, resolving within 1–2 weeks. Usually these symptoms are tolerated if appropriate explanation is given. However, if patients are not prepared, they may affect compliance with medication. A useful approach is either to initiate treatment with a very low dose or to cover the patient for a period of 1–2 weeks with a short-term prescription of a high-potency benzodiazepine such as clonazepam or alprazolam.

Most studies, so far, have addressed the question of short-term efficacy, usually up to 8–12 weeks. However, continuation of treatment with imipramine for more than 6 months appears to reduce relapse rates (Mavissakian and Perel 1992a, 1992b). Given the chronic, recurring nature of panic disorder and the associated disability, most authorities argue that the optimal length of treatment should be similar to that for depression. It is suggested that responders should continue medication for 12–24 months at full dose, before gradual tapering over a period of 4–6 months (Ballenger et al 1998a). A transient withdrawal syndrome, similar to the one described earlier for the SSRIs, also affects patients coming off tricyclics antidepressants (Haddad 1998).

Benzodiazepines

Alprazolam, a high-potency benzodiazepine, has been extensively studied in the acute treatment of panic disorder. It has shown efficacy equal to that of imipramine, and is significantly better than placebo. The improvement was evident in all major symptom areas, i.e. number of panic attacks and anticipatory anxiety and avoidance behaviour (Ballenger et al 1988, Andersch et al 1991). Longer-term studies showed that the improvement was maintained (Schweizer et al 1993). The usual amount given is 4–6 mg/day, divided into two or three doses, and the effect seems to correspond to the plasma levels achieved (Greenblatt et al 1993).

Although fewer studies have been conducted with other benzodiazepines, those tested show, on the whole, similar efficacy. They include the high-potency clonazepam (Tesar et al 1991) and lorazepam (Rickels and Schweizer 1986). The recommended dose for clonazepam is 1–2 mg/day (divided in two). The optimum dose of lorazepam is less clear. In studies, up to 7 mg/day was given, again in two or three doses. For the less potent benzodiazepines, such as diazepam, higher doses (up to 40 mg/day) are needed (Noyes et al 1996). As mentioned earlier, this class of drugs may also be of use during the early phase of treatment with an antidepressant.

The benzodiazepines are generally well tolerated and have more rapid onset of action than the antidepressants, with improvement seen even during the first week in some cases. The most common side effects include daytime sedation, fatigue and weakness, slurred speech, and subtle cognitive and memory impairment. Benzodiazepines have also been blamed for an increased risk of road traffic accidents and falls in elderly people (Lader 1999). The more potent benzodiazepines, compared with the less potent ones, offer a wider margin between clinically effective doses and doses that produce unwanted sedation (Argyropoulos et al 1999).

A lot of discussion has taken place in recent years about the issues of tolerance, dependence, withdrawal symptoms on discontinuation and the abuse potential of the benzodiazepines (Lader 1999). This resulted in adverse publicity and the generation of various national guidelines around the world, severely restricting the use of these drugs, or advocating them only for short-term treatments (Royal College of Physchiatrists 1997). Despite the undoubted problems, the worries over benzodiazepines seem to be excessive (Argyropoulos et al 1999). In the case of panic disorder, long-term studies with alprazolam have not shown evidence of tolerance and escalation of dose (American Psychiatric Association 1998). A similar study with clonazepam produced the same results (Worthington et al 1998).

Discontinuation is more of an issue, with a significant number of patients experiencing withdrawal symptoms, even after only 6–8 weeks of treatment. These withdrawal symptoms are almost universal if the drug is stopped abruptly. Tapering of the medication reduces the intensity of withdrawal but it does not always prevent its occurrence, especially towards the end of the taper (Schweizer et al 1990). Discontinuation problems with benzodiazepines are encountered more often than with antidepressants. Sometimes it is very difficult to distinguish between the withdrawal symptoms themselves and rebound/relapse of the original disorder (American Psychiatric Association 1998). It is possible that a higher propensity for withdrawal may be associated with higher relapse rates as well. The American Psychiatric Association (1998) advises gradual reduction of the medication, over a period of 2–4 months, at a rate no higher than 10% of the dose of the medication per week.

There is some evidence from long-term follow-up studies that patients on benzodiazepines may fare slightly worse than those on antidepressants. One study found that, after 8 months, patients on imipramine had a better symptomatic outcome than those on alprazolam (Curtis et al 1993). In a 3-year natural follow-up study, the percentage of patients still using alprazolam was double that of the patients taking imipramine (74% versus 32%) (Lepola 1993). Although this may well indicate poorer outcome or development of dependence and withdrawal difficulties, it is also possible that it reflects higher incidence of side effects with imipramine.

Monoamine oxidase inhibitors and reversible inhibitors of monoamine oxidase

Early studies, before the advent of the current classification systems, suggested that monoamine oxidase inhibitors (MAOIs) were effective in patients who currently would have been considered as having panic disorder (Sargant and Dally 1962). Since then, MAOIs (especially phenelzine) have been included in a number of studies and generally perform at least as well as the tricyclic antidepressants (Lydiard 1995). However, no studies with these drugs have been performed after the concept of panic disorder acquired its present form in the early 1980s (Rosenberg 1999). It is, therefore, difficult to comment on the widely held belief among clinicians that they are as good as, if not better than, other antidepressants in treating this condition.

The well-known dietary restrictions, potential lethality in overdose and the side effects in long-term use, such as hypotension, weight gain, insomnia, peripheral oedema and neuropathy, plus the risk of sympathomimetic potentiation, limit the use of these drugs. They may present a useful alternative in the hands of experts, however, as a second- or third-line options.

The introduction of the reversible inhibitors of monoamine oxidase-A (RIMAs) renewed interest in this class of agents. Their side-effect profile is much more favourable and usually no dietary restrictions are required. Furthermore, the new compounds, unlike the traditional MAOIs, can be used in combination with other antidepressants such as SSRIs without major problems (Joffe and Bakish 1994) although caution should always be exercised. Two drugs have been tested in this area: moclobemide, which already holds a licence for depression in many countries, and brofaromine. The latter, apart from its RIMA properties, is also a serotonin uptake blocker. So far, the results are conflicting. Two 8-week studies of moclobemide have been reported.

One indicated efficacy for moclobemide in panic disorder, whereas the other was negative (Tiller et al 1997, Loerch et al 1999). Interestingly, in the second study, although moclobemide was no better than placebo, it appeared to enhance the effect of concomitant cognitive–behavioural therapy. In a recent multicentre, parallel group, 1-year study comparing moclobemide with fluoxetine, both drugs were equally effective (Tiller et al 1999). Brofaromine, in a double-blind randomized comparison with clomipramine, also showed an anti-panic effect and improvement in measures of agoraphobia (Bakish et al 1993).

New antidepressants

Venlafaxine is a new antidepressant compound that blocks the reuptake of both serotonin and noradrenaline. Open studies suggest that it may be effective in panic disorder (Geracioti 1995, Papp et al 1998). The patients experienced a marked improvement with relatively low doses of venlafaxine, an average of 50–75 mg/day in the first and 47 mg/day in the second study. Data drawn from one site of a large multicentre, double-blind, placebo-controlled study added weight to the potential of this drug in treating panic disorder (Pollack et al 1996). In such a low-dose range, however, venlafaxine is thought to act as a pure SSRI.

Nefazodone is a weak SSRI with postsynaptic 5-HT$_2$-blocking properties. A large multicentre, double-blind, placebo-controlled trial has recently been completed. Although the full results have not been published yet, a preliminary report from this study shows that nefazodone was effective and well tolerated (Cassano et al 1999).

Mirtazapine blocks presynaptic α_2-auto- and heteroreceptors, and increases the release of both noradrenaline and serotonin. It is an effective antidepressant and a small open study suggests that it may prove to be effective in panic disorder as well (Carpenter et al 1999).

Buspirone

This 5-HT$_{1a}$ partial agonist, which is effective in generalized anxiety disorder, does not appear to have a similar effect in panic disorder. Even doses of about 60 mg/day performed far worse than alprazolam and no better than placebo (Sheehan et al 1993). Nevertheless, it may be of some value, augmenting the effect of cognitive–behavioural therapy (Bouvard et al 1997).

Other drugs

β Blockers

For some time, there was a widespread belief among clinicians that β blockers, by virtue of controlling the peripheral noradrenaline-mediated symptoms of panic, should be effective in this condition by reducing the anxiety associated with the attacks. The limited number of trials performed so far has not upheld this belief. These studies have produced mixed results in patients with symptoms of panic disorder or agoraphobia (Laufer and Weizman 1999). Some small crossover trials were positive, but, in a small double-blind crossover comparison with diazepam, propranolol was much less effective than the benzodiazepine (Noyes et al 1984). In a larger, double-blind comparison of the same β blocker with alprazolam and placebo, alprazolam was significantly better than propranolol, which in turn was no better than placebo (Munjack et al 1989). Another study comparing the same drugs found no difference between the two, other than the earlier onset of action of alprazolam (Ravaris et al 1991). The possible use of β blockers as augmentors of established treatments has not been properly tested. It is of note that some patients find the altered cardiac function resulting from these drugs anxiety provoking in itself, probably through a cognitive mechanism.

Calcium channel blockers

Drugs such as verapamil, nifedipine and diltiazem are thought to affect the cardiovascular symptoms that predominate panic attacks. Some small trials have indicated that they may be useful in treating panic disorder, although the clinical effect appears to be modest. There have also been some negative trials (Balon and Ramesh 1996, American Psychiatric Association 1998). Clearly, further evaluation of the calcium channel blockers in panic disorder is needed, because these drugs may prove to be useful adjuncts to established treatments, since they can be combined safely with most psychotropics.

Anticonvulsants

There is evidence from a crossover trial and uncontrolled trials that sodium valproate may be effective in panic disorder, whereas carbamazepine is not (Laufer and Weizman 1999). More rigorous studies are needed to confirm the efficacy of sodium valproate. Gabapentin is a new anticonvulsant with an unclear mechanism of action. A recent double-blind, placebo-controlled study of gabapentin in doses up to 3,600 mg/day indicated that this drug may have anti-panic effects (Pande et al 2000).

Clonidine

Clonidine appears to have an acute anxiolytic effect in patients with panic disorder, but this is mostly transient (Udhe et al 1989, Laufer and Weizman 1999). This may reflect the development of tolerance.

Antipsychotics

Low doses of antipsychotics are occasionally used for the treatment of anxiety. Early studies in panic disorder were negative (Laufer and Weizman 1999). Antipsychotics also pose the risk of akathisia and extrapyramidal side effects in acute treatment, and tardive dyskinesia with chronic use.

Anxiolytics in development

Partial agonists of benzodiazepine receptors

As discussed earlier in this chapter, benzodiazepines are effective anti-panic agents but their use poses a number of problems. The currently available compounds are highly selective full agonists of the GABA–benzodiazepine receptor-complex, where they act to modulate the actions of GABA. It has been postulated that the development of partial agonists for this receptor site may offer significant advantages over the classic drugs. In theory, the partial agonists should cause less tolerance and withdrawal, have no liability for abuse and they should not potentiate the effects of ethanol. On the other hand, they are likely to be less effective than the traditional benzodiazepines. A number of such benzodiazepine-receptor partial agonists are currently being tested in clinical trials for panic disorder and other anxiety indications. These new drugs are either benzodiazepine derivatives or have a different chemical structure (imidazopyridines and β carbolines). One such partial agonist, pagoclone, has shown some promising early results in panic disorder (Hood et al 2000).

Drugs acting on serotonin receptors

The identification of a multiplicity of serotonin receptors, and the development of specific agonists and antagonists for these receptors, offer the possibility of new treatments, as well as facilitating the clarification of the role of this neurotransmitter in anxiety. A number of compounds that bind specifically to 5-HT_{1a}, 5-HT_{2a} and 5-HT_3 receptors are currently undergoing trials for anxiety disorders (Hood et al 2000). Although gepirone, a 5-HT_{1a} partial agonist, has shown some promising results in an open study in panic disorder, the picture with ondansetron, a 5-HT_3 antagonist, does not look very positive (Pencknold et al 1993, Schneier et al 1996). However, it is too early to have a clear idea whether these or other serotonin receptor-specific drugs will prove to be useful anti-panic agents.

Drugs acting on neuropeptide receptors

The neuropeptide field has been an area of very active research in recent years. Evidence is accumulating that a number of them may play a significant role in the regulation of human anxiety, either alone or in conjunction with the classic neurotransmitters GABA, serotonin and noradrenaline (Griebel 1999).

Trials with specific neuropeptide receptor ligands have started to emerge, but there has been no breakthrough as yet. Antagonists of the cholecystokinin-B (CCK-B) receptor have been disappointing to date. Double-blind, placebo-controlled trials of two such compounds (L-365,260 and CI-988) in panic disorder were negative (Kramer et al 1995, Pande et al 1999). However, the pharmacokinetic properties of these compounds have been questioned, and their ability to cross the blood–brain barrier is unclear. Better preparations are needed before it can be decided whether CCK-B antagonists have a role to play in the treatment of panic.

At the same time, antagonists of corticotrophin-releasing factor (CRF) are undergoing evaluation. It is postulated that agonists of the Y-1 receptor type of neuropeptide Y (NPY) may be anxiolytics; however, no useful ligands have been put forward yet (Griebel 1999). Research with substance P antagonists appears more promising at the moment. One such compound, MK-869, was reported to have antidepressant properties. In the same study, it was noticed that it significantly improved anxiety measures in depressed patients, but it was later withdrawn from development. Other, more potent, substance P antagonists are currently on trial. It remains to be seen whether they will prove to be effective anxiolytics (Nutt 1998).

Inositol

L-Myoinositol (inositol) is a natural isomer of glucose that forms part of our normal diet. It is also a precursor of the intracellular phosphoinositol cycle. Several neurotransmitters, including serotonin and noradrenaline, act on this second messenger system via some of their postsynaptic receptors. It is therefore postulated that externally ingested inositol exerts its behavioural effects beyond the synaptic level, where the currently used psychotropics are thought to act. A small (21 patients), double-blind, crossover, placebo-controlled trial was performed in panic disorder (Benjamin et al 1995). The patients were treated for 4 weeks with the active compound and for a further 4 weeks with either mannitol or glucose (which appear identical), which played the role of placebo. The dose of inositol used was 12 g/day, given as a powder dissolved in juice. The trial was successful, in that the patients experienced reduction in the frequency and severity of their panic attacks and the severity of their agoraphobia, and this reduction was significantly more than with placebo. There were no significant side effects and the drug was generally very well tolerated.

The results need, of course, to be replicated in larger samples and in direct comparison with established treatments. The preparation of the drug is problematic; the sheer volume of what needs to be ingested may put patients off and this has to be solved before it becomes a viable alternative to established anxiolytics. However, the fact that inositol is a natural component of our diet makes it potentially very attractive as a therapeutic option.

Psychological treatments

Cognitive–behavioural therapy

This brief (usually around 12 sessions) psychotherapeutic approach incorporates a number of different treatment aspects (Table 16), all of which are thought to help bring about improvement. Apart from education on the nature of panic disorder and its symptoms, it uses pen and paper techniques (e.g. in the form of diaries) to monitor the progress of specific antecedents, emotional and cognitive reactions, and the resulting symptoms of panic and/or avoidance behaviour. The bulk of the cognitive work consists of the identification and countering of catastrophic misinterpretations, arising mainly from over-estimation of bodily sensations. Practical anxiety management techniques, such as breathing exercises, are advocated when appropriate. Finally, a behavioural element, based on graded exposure to avoided situations, is employed to counter agoraphobia (American Psychiatric Association 1998).

This form of psychological treatment has been greatly refined and operationalized in recent years. When patients are given a free choice, it appears to be the preferred option for them, ahead of medication. A number of patients (10–30%), however, are unable or unwilling to conform to the demands of the treatment. It requires the active participation of the patient, and sometimes that of his or her partner, with a lot of work to be done at home or during everyday outdoor activities. It is, therefore, quite time-consuming. 'Side effects' in the traditional sense of those seen with medications do not exist. However, exposure increases anxiety, at least initially. Dependence on the therapist may develop, as in other forms of therapy (American Psychiatric Association 1998, Chosak et al 1999).

Psycho-education and monitoring	Cognitive restucturing	Anxiety management techiques	Exposure
1 discussion on the nature of panic	1 identification of catastrophic thoughts	1 breathing exercises	1 graded interoceptive exposure to somatic sensations produced in the treatment room, such as hyper-ventilation
2 link of somatic symptoms and fear component	2 link of thoughts with somatic sensations	2 muscle relaxation	
3 explanation of the treatment	3 countering of overestimating of somatic symptoms		2 in vivo exposure to feared and avoided stimuli/ situations
4 monitoring symptoms and progress with diaries	4 development of alternative explanations		

Table 16
Components of cognitive–behavioural therapy (CBT) in panic disorder

Over 10 randomized studies have confirmed the short-term (up to 16 weeks) efficacy of cognitive–behavioural therapy (CBT) in panic disorder and agoraphobia. These studies, by their nature, usually include smaller numbers than multicentre trials of medication, but they are of comparable scientific rigour. As with pharmacological treatments, all major symptom areas improve: panic attacks, anticipatory anxiety and avoidant behaviour. Some studies have also addressed the issue of using only some components of the model, taking a more cognitive or more behavioural approach. Although each one shows efficacy in its own right, a combined approach is thought to be more robust. The advantage of a more limited intervention may rest in cases where the patient does not exhibit the full array of symptoms, e.g. using exposure for agoraphobia without clinically significant panic attacks. This illustrates the fundamental philosophy of CBT, which, in contrast with psychodynamically orientated therapies, aspires to remain focused on the problem in hand, i.e. the patient's symptoms, rather than expand to a wholesale 'in-depth' psychological treatment (American Psychiatric Association 1998, Chosak et al 1999). This narrow focus has allowed CBT to be tested rigorously and successfully and, by virtue of its brief nature, it has also turned it into the preferred therapy for patients, therapists and service purchasers alike. On the other hand, it attracts criticism from the advocates of more holistic approaches.

Long-term studies, of at least 1 year's duration and sometimes more, show that the treatment gains are largely maintained. There is evidence that improvement of avoidance and agoraphobia persists for up to 8 years. Sometimes booster sessions are needed, if short-term symptomatic relapse occurs. The assertion by some advocates of CBT that the long-term picture with this treatment is better than with medication, in that it offers more protection against relapses, is not, however, substantiated. When patients are examined more closely for their symptoms and functioning, between assessment points, a substantial number show a fluctuating picture, from disorder-free status to significant and disabling pathology (Brown and Barlow 1995). This probably reflects the recurring nature of the disorder itself and the difficulty in achieving a 'cure', rather than the failure of one treatment modality or another. The use of CBT requires some expertise, so its use is limited by the continuing scarcity of properly trained therapists, especially within the National Health Service.

Finally, CBT has been used successfully, as an adjunct treatment, in helping panic disorder patients to discontinue benzodiazepine medication, and minimize early relapse (Spiegel et al 1994, American Psychiatric Association 1998).

Other psychological treatments

Group therapy, along cognitive–behavioural lines, has been used successfully to treat panic disorder, although fewer studies have been performed compared with individual CBT. Psychodynamic psychotherapy also claims efficacy, but research in this area is very difficult. There are case reports of successful treatments and some preliminary positive studies have been reported, while more are currently under way. Patient support groups are considered helpful, especially in providing psychoeducation and facilitating exposure (American Psychiatric Association 1998).

Drugs versus psychotherapy

Important problems in the interpretation of research in panic disorder treatments

The establishment of operational criteria for the diagnosis of panic disorder was followed by an attempt for a more unified approach in research – pharmacological or psychological. The selection of the most relevant clinical and social aspects of the condition, and the choice of appropriate outcome measures for them, which should be used in as many studies as possible, would lead to an easier interpretation of the results and a more general applicability of the findings. Various consensus panels of experts have tried to address this issue in recent years. Despite their efforts and the production of guidelines, the situation is still not satisfactory, so it is sometimes difficult to determine the relative merits of different treatments (Weise et al 1996).

Another problem is the placebo response rates which in some trials in panic disorder, are exceptionally high and may mask the true treatment response rates (Piercy et al 1996) Better designed studies, with careful procedural standardization and patient selection, may help to reduce placebo rates to levels comparable to those seen in schizophrenia or bipolar disorder. A reanalysis of the combined data from two large multicentre treatment trials, comparing sertraline with placebo, showed that patients who 'responded' to placebo experienced symptomatic relief, but had no improvement in quality-of-life measures (Rapaport et al 2000). This was in contrast to the improvement produced by the medication, which was evident across both the clinical and the social dimension of the illness. Systematic assessment of quality of life may, therefore, help in differentiating drug from placebo response. However, it may be that panic disorder, by its nature, is more likely to yield a higher placebo response than psychotic disorders. The usually unsatisfactory comparable placebo methods when drugs are tested against psychological therapies, or even when psychological therapies are tested alone, also sometimes make the interpretation of the results of such studies very difficult.

Another criticism levelled at randomized controlled trials is that the results are not easily generalized, because the study population is not representative of the average everyday patient encountered in general practice or an outpatient psychiatric clinic. It is true that exclusion criteria in medication or psychotherapy trials produce a rarefied or 'sanitized' sample, but this is not easy to circumvent. Studies of the effectiveness of various treatments in clinical practice, as opposed to their efficacy in trials, will hopefully solve this problem.

Monotherapy or combination of drugs and psychotherapy?

The old question of biological (medication) versus psychotherapeutic approach still divides theorists, researchers, clinicians and patients. Inevitably, perhaps, studies showing one or the other approach to be superior have been reported. However, the overall picture is one of equal efficacy of medication and CBT in panic disorder, in both short- and long-term studies. Unless there are specific reasons to favour one modality over the other, such as availability, previous response, strong patient preference, or treatment failures and unacceptable side effects, both options should be kept open, and the management plan should be tailored to the needs of the individual patient.

Some clinicians consider the combination of pharmacological and psychological treatments (especially CBT) as the optimal regimen for anxiety disorders. Currently, this is reserved for the more severe cases that fail to respond to either treatment alone. Some studies indicate an advantage for the combined approach, whereas others failed to do so (American Psychiatric Association 1998). A large multicentre trial, sponsored by the National Institutes of Mental Health (NIMH) in the USA, studying the combination of imipramine and CBT in panic disorder, has recently been completed, and the results are awaited with interest. In meta-analyses of the efficacy of medication in panic disorder, CBT or a combination in short-term and long-term studies, the combination appears to be significantly better than monotherapy, especially for the outcome of agoraphobia (van Balkom et al 1997, Bakker et al 1998). As agoraphobia is the strongest clinical predictor of outcome (see chapter on Course and prognosis), it is sensible to recommend that a combination treatment should be used more often or earlier in treatment (van Balkom and van Dyck 1998).

Finally, the concomitant use of benzodiazepines has been of some concern for behavioural therapists who believe that it may reduce the efficacy of their therapy. A study of a group of people with severe chronic agoraphobia found no evidence that the outcome of behavioural therapy was significantly affected by the concurrent use of diazepam (Wardle et al 1994). Furthermore, there was no evidence for relapse or loss of treatment gains on withdrawal from the drug over 1 year of follow-up. Benzodiazepines, if judiciously used, may facilitate the participation to exposure of patients whose initial anxiety levels are too high to allow confrontation with the avoided situation.

Summary

A number of effective treatments are currently available for panic disorder and agoraphobia. These include medications, notably the SSRIs, tricyclic antidepressants and some benzodiazepines, and cognitive–behavioural therapy. The choice depends on availability, familiarity with the treatment, patient preference, comorbidity of depression and previously successful treatment.

Panic and agoraphobia may run a recurring course, which can prove severely disabling if not treated properly. Some patients, therefore, require long-term treatment, which may extend beyond 1 year.

We have summarized our suggestions for a rational treatment of panic disorder as an algorithm in Figure 13.

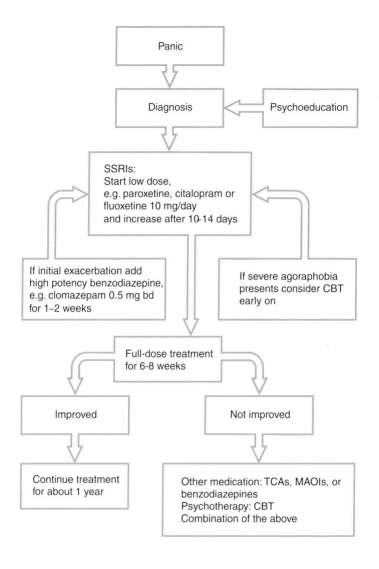

Figure 13

Algorithm for treatment of panic disorder. TCAs, tricyclic antidepressants; MAOIs, monoamine oxidase inhibitors; CBT, cognitive–behavioural therapy; SSRIs, selective serotonin reuptake inhibitors.

References

American Psychiatric Association. *Diagnostic and Statistical Manual of Mental Disorders*, 3rd edn. Washington DC: American Psychiatric Association, 1980.

American Psychiatric Association. *Diagnostic and Statistical Manual of Mental Disorders*, 4th edn. Washington DC: American Psychiatric Association, 1994.

American Psychiatric Association. Practice guideline for the treatment of patients with panic disorder. *Am J Psychiatry* 1998; **155**(suppl): 1–34.

Andersch S, Rosenberg NK, Kullingsjo H et al. Efficacy and safety of alprazolam, imipramine and placebo in treating panic disorder: a Scandnavian multicenter study. *Acta Psychiatr Scandin* 1991; suppl 365: 18–27.

Andrews G, Stewart G, Allen R, Henderson AS. The genetics of six neurotic disorders: a twin study. *J Affect Disord* 1990; **19**: 23–9.

Angst J. Depression and anxiety: implications for nosology, course, and treatment. *J Clin Psychiatry* 1997; **58**(suppl 8): 3–5.

Angst J, Merikangas KR, Preisig M. Subthreshold syndromes of depression and anxiety in the community. *J Clin Psychiatry* 1997; **58**(suppl 8): 6–10.

Argyropoulos SV, Nutt DJ. The use of benzodiazepines in anxiety and other disorders. *Eur Neuropsychopharmacol* 1999; **9**(suppl 6): S407–12.

Bakish D, Saxena BM, Bowen D, D'Souza J. Reversible monoamine oxidase-A inhibitors in panic disorder. *Clin Neuropsychopharmacol* 1993; **16**(suppl 2): S77–82.

Bakker A, van Balkom AJLM, Spinhoven PH et al. Follow-up on the treatment of panic disorder with or without agoraphobia: a review. J Nerv Ment Dis 1998; **186:** 414–19.

Bakker A, van Dyck R, Spinhoven P, van Balkom AJ. Paroxetine, clomipramine, and cognitive therapy in the treatment of panic disorder. *J Clin Psychiatry* 1999; **60:** 831–8.

Ballenger JC. Selective serotonin reuptake inhibitors (SSRIs) in panic disorder. In: Nutt DJ, Ballenger JC, Lepine J-P, eds, *Panic Disorder: Clinical diagnosis, management and mechanisms.* London: Martin Dunitz, 1999: 159–78.

Ballenger JC, Burrows GD, DuPont RL et al. Alprazolam in panic disorder and agoraphobia: results from a multicenter trial. *Arch Gen Psychiatry* 1988; **45:** 413–22.

Ballenger JC, Davidson JRT, Lecrubier Y et al. Consensus statement on panic disorder from the international consensus group on depression and anxiety. *J Clin Psychiatry* 1998a; **59**(suppl. 8): 47–54.

Ballenger JC, Wheadon DE, Steiner M et al. Double-blind, fixed-dose, placebo-controlled study of paroxetine in the treatment of panic disorder. *Am J Psychiatry* 1998b; **155:** 36–42.

Balon R, Ramesh C. Calcium channel blockers for anxiety disorders? *Ann Clin Psychiatry* 1996; **8:** 215–20.

Balon R, Pohl R, Yeragani VK et al. Follow-up study of control subjects with lactate and isoprotenerol induced panic attacks. *Am J Psychiatry* 1988; **145:** 238–41.

Barlow DH. *Anxiety and its Disorders: The Nature and Treatment of Anxiety and Panic.* New York: The Guilford Press, 1998.

Barsky AJ, Barnett MC, Clearly PD. Hypochondriasis and panic disorder. Boundary and overlap. *Arch Gen Psychiatry* 1994; **51:** 918–25.

Beitman BD, Basha I, Flaker G et al. Atypical or nonanginal chest pain: panic disorder or coronary artery disease. *Ann Intern Med* 1987; **147:** 1548–52.

Bell CJ, Nutt DJ. Serotonin and panic. *Br J Psychiatry* 1998; **172:** 465–71.

Benjamin J, Levine J, Fux M et al. Double-blind, placebo-controlled, crossover trial of inositol treatment for panic disorder. *Am J Psychiatry* 1995; **152:** 1084–6.

Berrios GE, Link C. Anxiety disorders. In: Berrios GE, Porter R, eds, *A History of Clinical Psychiatry*. London: The Athlone Press, 1995: 545–62.

Bouvard M, Mollard E, Guerin J, Cottreaux J. Study and course of the psychological profile in 77 patients expressing panic disorder with agoraphobia after cognitive behaviour therapy with or without buspirone. *Psychother Psychosomatics* 1997; **66:** 27–32.

Boyer W. Serotonin uptake inhibitors are superior to imipramine and alprazolam in alleviating panic attacks: a meta-analysis. *Int Clin Psychopharmacol* 1995; **10:** 45–9.

Bradwejn J, Koszyski D, Couetoux du Terre A et al. The panicogenic effects of cholecystokinin tetrapeptide are antagonised by L-365,260, a central cholecystokinin receptor antagonist, in patients with panic disorder. *Arch Gen Psychiatry* 1994; **51:** 486–93.

Broadhead W, Blazer D, George L, Tse C. Depression, disability days and days lost from work in a prospective epidemiological survey. *JAMA* 1990; **264:** 2524–8.

Brown TA, Barlow DH. Long term outcome of cognitive behavioral treatment of panic disorder. *J Consult Clin Psychol* 1995; **63:** 754–65.

Carpenter LL, Leon Z, Yasmin S, Price LH. Clinical experience with mirtazapine in the treatment of panic disorder. *Ann Clin Psychiatry* 1999; **11:** 81–6.

Carter JD, Joyce PR, Mulder RT et al. Gender differences in the rate of comorbid axis I disorders in depressed outpatients. *Depr Anxiety* 1999; **9:** 49–53.

Cassano G, Benkert O, Wade A et al. A multicentre, double-blind comparison of nefazodone and placebo in the treatment of panic disorder. *Eur Neuropsychopharmacol* 1999; **9**(suppl 5): S250.

Cassano GB, Michelini S, Shear MK et al. The panic-agoraphobic spectrum: a descriptive approach to the assessment and treatment of subtle symptoms. *Am J Psychiatry* 1997; **154**(suppl 6): 27–38.

Chosak A, Baker SL, Thorn GR et al. Psychological treatments of panic disorder. In: Nutt DJ, Ballenger JC, Lepine J-P, eds, *Panic Disorder. Clinical diagnosis, management and mechanisms*. London: Martin Dunitz, 1999: 203–19.

Clark DM. A cognitive model of panic. In: Rachman S, Maser JD, eds, *Panic, Psychological Perspectives*. Hillsdale NJ: Lawrence Erlabaum, 1988: 71–89.

Coplan JD, Sharma T, Rosenblum LA et al. Effects of sodium lactate infusion on the cisternal lactate and carbon dioxide levels in nonhuman primates. *Am J Psychiatry* 1992; **149:** 1369–73.

Cowley DS, Fliok SN, Roy-Byrne PP. Long-term course and outcome in panic disorder: a naturalistic follow-up study. *Anxiety* 1996; **2:** 13–21.

Curtis GC, Massana J, Udina C et al. Maintenance drug therapy of panic disorder. *J Psychiat Res* 1993; **27**(suppl 1): 127–42.

Dager SR, Strauss WL, Marro KI et al. Proton magnetic spectroscopy investigation of hyperventilation in subjects with panic disorder and comparison subjects. *Am J Psychiatry* 1995; **152:** 666–72.

Den Boer JA, Westenberg HG. Effect of a serotonin and noradrenaline uptake inhibitor in panic disorder: a double-blind comparative study with fluvoxamine and maprotiline. *Int Clin Psychopharmacol* 1988; **3:** 59–74.

DuPont RL, Rice DP, Miller LS et al. Economic costs of anxiety disorders. *Anxiety* 1996; **2:** 167–72.

Eaton WW, Drymon A, Weissman MM. Panic and phobias. In: Robbins LN, Regier DA, eds, *Psychiatric Disorders in America: The epidemiologic catchment area study*. New York: The Free Press, 1991: 155–79.

Eaton WW, Kessler RC, Wittchen HU, Magee WJ. Panic and panic disorder in the United States. *Am J Psychiatry* 1994; **151:** 413–20.

Fahy TJ, O'Rourke D, Brophy J et al. The Galway Study of panic disorder. I: Clomipramine and lofepramine in DSM III-R panic disorder: a placebo controlled trial. *J Affect Dis* 1992; **25:** 63–75.

Faravelli C, Paionni A. Panic disorder: clinical course, etiology and prognosis. In: Nutt DJ, Ballenger JC, Lepine J-P, eds, *Panic Disorder: Clinical diagnosis, management and mechanisms*. London: Martin Dunitz, 1999: 25–44.

Faravelli CP, Panichi C, Pallanti S et al. Perception of parenting style in panic and agoraphobia. *Acta Psychiat Scandin* 1991; **84:** 6–8.

Frances A, Manning D, Marin D et al. Relationship of anxiety and depression. *Psychopharmacology* 1992; **106:** S82–6.

Freud S. The justification for the detaching from neurasthenia a particular syndrome: anxiety neurosis. In: *The Collected Papers*, Volume 1. London: Hogarth Press, 1953: 76–106.

Fyer AJ. Anxiety disorders:genetics. In: Kaplan HI, Sadock BJ, Sadock VA, eds, *The Comprehensive Textbook of Psychiatry*, 7th edn. New York: Lippincott, Williams & Wilkins: 2000.

Fyer AJ, Katon W, Hollifield M et al. The DSM-IV panic disorder field trial: panic attack frequency and functional disability. *Anxiety* 1996; **2:** 157–66.

Geracioti TD. Venlafaxine treatment of panic disorder: a case series. *J Clin Psychiatry* 1995; **56:** 408–10.

Goddard AW, Woods SW, Sholomskas DE et al. Effects of the serotonin reuptake inhibitor fluvoxamine. *Psychiat Res* 1993; **48:** 119–33.

Goisman RM, Washaw MG, Peterson LG et al. Panic, agoraphobia and panic disorder with agoraphobia data from a multicentre anxiety disorders study. *J Nerv Ment Dis* 1994; **182:** 72–9.

Gorman JM. Comorbid depression and anxiety spectrum disorders. *Depr Anxiety* 1996/1997; **4:** 160–8.

Gorman JM, Kent JM, Sullivan GM, Coplan JD. Neuroanatomical hypothesis of panic disorder, revised. *Am J Psychiatry* 2000; **157:** 493–505.

Greenblatt DJ, Harmatiz JS, Shader RI. Plasma alprazolam concentrations: relation to efficacy and side effects in the treatment of panic disorder. *Arch Gen Psychiatry* 1993; **50:** 715–22.

Griebel G. Is there a future for neuropeptide receptor ligands in the treatment of anxiety disorders? *Pharm Therapeutics* 1999; **82:** 1–61.

Haddad P. The SSRI discontinuation syndrome. *J Psychopharmacol* 1998; **12:** 305–13.

Hamilton M. The clinical distinction between anxiety and depression. *Br J Clin Pharmacology* 1983; **15:** 165S–9S.

Hoehn-Saric R, McLeod DR, Hipsley PA. Effect of fluvoxamine on panic disorder. *J Clin Psychopharmacol* 1993; **13:** 321–6.

Hollifield M, Katon W, Skipper B et al. Panic disorder and quality of life: variables predictive of functional impairment. *Am J Psychiatry* 1997; **154:** 766–72.

Hood SD, Argyropoulos SV, Nutt DJ. Agents in development for anxiety disorders. *CNS Drugs* 2000; **13:** 421–31.

Horwath E, Lish J, Johnson J et al. Agoraphobia without panic: Clinical re-appraisal of an epidemiological finding. *Am J Psychiatry* 1993; **150:** 1496.

Jakubec DF, Taylor CB. Medical aspects of panic disorder and its relationship to other conditions. In: Nutt DJ, Ballenger JC, Lopine JP, eds, *Panic Disorder: Clinical diagnosis, management and mechanisms.* London: Martin Dunitz, 1999: 109–24.

Joffe RT, Bakish D. Combined SSRI-moclobemide treatment of psychiatric illness. *J Clin Psychiatry* 1994; **55:** 24–5.

Katerndahl DA, Realini JP. Quality of life and panic-related work disability in subjects with infrequent panic and panic disorder. *J Clin Psychiatry* 1997; **58:** 153–8.

Katon W, Hollifield M, Chapman T et al. Infrequent panic attacks: psychiatric comorbidity, personal characterisitics and functional disability. *J Psych Research* 1995; **29:** 121–31.

Katschnig H, Amering M. The long-term course of panic disorder and its predictors. *J Clin Psychopharmacol* 1998; **18**(suppl. 2): 6S–11S.

Katschnig H, Amering M, Stolk JM, Ballenger JC. Predictors of quality of life in a long-term follow-up study in panic disorder patients after a clinical drug trial. *Psychopharm Bulletin* 1996; **32:** 149–55.

Katschnig H, Amering M, Stolk JM et al. Long-term follow-up after a drug trial for panic disorder. *Br J Psychiatry* 1995; **167:** 487–94.

Keller MB, Yonkers KA, Warshaw MG et al. Remission and relapse in subjects with panic disorder and panic with agoraphobia. *J Nerv Mental Dis* 1994; **182:** 290–6.

Kendler KS, Neale MC, Kessler RC et al. Panic disorder in women: A population-based twin study. *Psychol Med* 1993; **23:** 397–406.

Kessler RC, Nelson CB, McGonagle KA et al. Comorbidity of DSM-III-R major depressive disorder in the general population: results from the US National Comorbidity Survey. *Br J Psychiatry* 1996; **168**(suppl 30): 17–30.

Kim JJ, Fanselow MS. Modality–specific retrograde amnesia of fear. *Science* 1992; **256:** 675–7.

Klein DF. Delineation of two drug-responsive anxiety syndromes, *Psychopharmacologia* 1964; **5:** 397–408.

Klein DF. Anxiety reconceptualised. In: Klein DF, Rabkin JG, eds, *New Research and Changing Concepts*, New York: Raven Press, 1981.

Klein DF. False suffocation alarms, spontaneous panics, and related conditions. *Arch Gen Psychiatry* 1993; **50:** 306–17.

Kloss RJ, Cameron O. Comorbidity of anxiety with depression: do primary and secondary anxiety differ? In: Burrows GD, Roth M Sir, Noyes R Jr, eds, *Handbook of Anxiety*, Volume 5. Amsterdam: Elsevier Science Publishers, 1992; 161–79.

Kramer MS, Cutler NR, Ballenger JC et al. A placebo-controlled trial of L-365,260, a CCK-B antagonist, in panic disorder. *Biol Psychiatry* 1995; **37:** 462–6.

Lader MH. Limitations on the use of benzodiazepines in anxiety and insomnia: are they justified? *Eur Neuropshychopharmacol* 1999; **9**(suppl 6): S399–405.

Laufer N, Weizman A. Other drug treatments and augmentation therapies for panic disorder. In: Nutt DJ, Ballenger JC, Lepine J-P, eds, *Panic Disorder. Clinical diagnosis, management and mechanisms*. London: Martin Dunitz, 1999: 179–202.

Lecrubier Y, Bakker A, Dunbar G, Judge R. A comparison of paroxetine, clomipramine and placebo in the treatment of panic disorder. *Acta Psychiat Scandin* 1997; **95:** 145–52.

Lecrubier Y, Judge R. Long-term evaluation of paroxetine, clomipramine and placebo in panic disorder. *Acta Pscyh Scand* 1997; **95:** 153–60.

Lelliot P, Marks I, McNamee G, Tobena A. Onset of panic disorder with agoraphobia. *Arch Gen Psychiatry* 1989; **46:**1000–4.

Lepine J-P, Pelissolo A. Epidemiology, comorbidity and genetics of panic disorder. In: Nutt DJ, Ballenger JC, Lepine J-P, eds, *Panic Disorder: Clinical diagnosis, management and mechanisms*. London: Martin Dunitz, 1999: 9–25.

Lepola UM, Rimon RH, Riekkinen PJ. Three-year follow-up of patients with panic disorder after short-term treatment with alprazolam and imipramine. *Int Clin Psychopharmacol* 1993; **8:** 115–18.

Lepola UM, Wade AG, Leinonen EV et al. A controlled, prospective, 1-year trial of citalopram in the treamtment of panic disorder. *J Clin Psychiatry* 1998; **59:** 528–34.

Loerch B, Graf-Morgenstern M, Hautzinger M et al. Randomised placebo-controlled trial of moclobemide, cognitive-behavioral therapy and their combination in panic disorder with agoraphobia. *Br J Psychiatry* 1999; **174:** 205–12.

Londborg PD, Wolkow R, Smith WT et al. Sertraline in the treatment of panic disorder. A multi-site, double-blind, placebo-controlled, fixed-dose investigation. *Br J Psychiatry* 1998; **173:** 54–60.

Lydiard RB. Drug treatment of panic disorder. *Bailliere Clin Psychiatry* 1995; **1:** 427–46.

Lydiard RB, Morton WA, Emmanuel MP et al. Preliminary report: placebo-controlled, double-blind study of the clinical and metabolic effects of desipramine in panic disorder. *Psychopharmacol Bull* 1993; **29:** 183–8.

Malizia AL, Nutt DJ. Brain mechanisms and circuits in panic disorder. In: Nutt DJ, Ballenger JC, Lepine J-P, eds, *Panic Disorder: Clinical diagnosis, management and mechanisms*. London: Martin Dunitz, 1999: 55–77.

Malizia AL, Cunningham VJ, Nutt DJ. Flumazenil delivery changes in panic disorder at rest. *Neuroimage* 1997; **5:** S302.

Margraf J, Taylor CB, Ehlers A et al. Panic attacks in the natural environment. *J Nerv Ment Dis* 1987; **175:** 558–65.

Markowitz JS, Weissman MM, Quellette R et al. Quality of life in panic disorder. *Arch Gen Psychiatry* 1989, **46:** 984–92.

Mavissakalian M, Perel JM. Clinical experiments in maintenance and discontinuation of imipramine therapy in panic disorder with agoraphobia. *Arch Gen Psychiatry* 1992a; **49:** 318–23.

Mavissakalian M, Perel JM. Protective effects of imipramine maintenance reatment in panic disorder with agoraphobia. *Am J Psychiatry* 1992b; **149:** 1053–7.

McNally RJ, Lorenz M. Anxiety sensitivity in agoraphobics. *J Behav Ther Exp Psychiatry* 1987; **18:** 3–11.

Michelson D, Lydiard RB, Pollack MH et al. Outcome assessment and clinical improvement in panic disorder: evidence from a randomised controlled trial of fluoxetine and placebo. *Am J Psychiatry* 1998; **155:** 1570–7.

Michelson D, Pollack M, Lydiard RB et al. Continuing treatment of panic disorder after acute response: randomised, placebo-controlled trial with fluoxetine. *Br J Psychiatry* 1999: **174:** 213–18.

Middleton HC. 'Psychological inflammation'. Clarification of the model and a rejoinder. *J Psychopharmacol* 1991; **5:** 301–4.

Modigh K, Westberg P, Eriksson E. Superiority of clomipramine over imipramine in the treatment of panic disorder: a placebo controlled trial. *J Clin Psychopharmacol* 1992; **12:** 251–61.

Munjack DJ, Crocker B, Cabe D et al. Alprazolam, propranolol, and placebo in the treatment of panic disorder and agoraphobia with panic attacks. J Clin Psychopharmacol 1989; **9:** 22–7.

Myers JK, Weissman MM, Tischler GL et al. Six-month prevalence of psychiatric disorders in three communities. *Arch Gen Psychiatry* 1984; **41:** 959–67.

Nemeroff CB. The HPA axis and the pathophysiology of depression: the role of early adverse experience. *J Psychopharmacology* 2000; 14 (suppl): A4.

Noyes R Jr, Anderson DJ, Clancy J et al. Diazepam and propranolol in panic disorder and agoraphobia. *Arch Gen Psychiatry* 1984: **41:** 287–92.

Noyes R Jr, Reich J, Clancy J, Gorman J. Reduction in hypochondriasis with treatment of panic disorder. *Br J Psychiatry* 1986; **149:** 631–5.

Noyes R Jr, Burrows GD, Reich JH et al. Diazepam versus alprazolam for the treatment of panic disorder. *J Clin Psychiatry* 1996; **57:** 349–55.

Nutt DJ. Substance P antagonists: a new treatment for depression? *Lancet* 1998; **352:** 1644–6.

Nutt DJ Bell CJ. Pactical pharmacotherapy for anxiety. *Adv Psychiat Treat* 1997; **3:** 79–85.

Nutt DJ, Glue P, Lawson CW, Wilson SJ. Flumazenil provocation of panic attacks: evidence for altered benzodiazepine receptor sensitivity in panic disorder. *Arch Gen Psychiatry* 1990; **47:** 917–25.

Oehrberg S, Christiansen PE, Behnke K. Paroxetine in the treatment of panic disorder: a randomised double-blind placebo-controlled study. *Br J Psychiatry* 1995; **167:** 374–9.

Olfson M, Fireman B, Weissman MM et al. Mental disorders and disability among patients in a primary care group practice. *Am J Psychiatry* 1997; **154:** 1734–40.

Ontiveros A, Fontaine R, Breton G et al. Correlation of severity of panic disorder and neuroanatomical changes on magnetic resonance imaging. *J Neuropsych Clin Neurosci* 1989; **1:** 404–8.

Pande AC, Greiner M, Adams JB et al, Placebo-controlled trial of the CCK-B antagonist, CI-988, in panic disorder. *Biol Psychiatry* 1999, **40.** 860–2.

Pande AC, Pollack MH, Crockatt J et al. Placebo-controlled study of gabapentin treatment of panic disorder. *J Clin Psychopharmacol* 2000; **20:** 467–71.

Papp LA, Sinha SS, Martinez JM et al. Low-dose venlafaxine treatment in panic disorder. Psychopharmacol Bull 1998; **34:** 207–9.

Parker G. Reported parental characteristics of agoraphobics and social phobics. *Br J Psychiatry* 1979; **135:** 555–60.

Parker G, Turpling H, Brown LB. A parental bonding instrument. *Brit J Med Psychol* 1975; **52:** 1–11.

Pencknold JC, Luthe L, Scott-Fleury M-H, Jenkins S. Gepirone and the treatment of panic disorder: an open study. *J Clin Psychopharmacol* 1993; **13:** 145–9.

Piercy MA, Sramek JJ, Cutler NR. Placebo response in anxiety disorders. *Ann Pharmacother* 1996; **30:** 1013–19.

Pine DS, Weese-Mayer DE, Silvestri JM et al. Anxiety and congenital hypoventilation syndrome. *Am J Psychiatry* 1994; **151:** 864–70.

Pitts FM, McClure JN. Lactate metabolism in anxiety neurosis. *N Engl J Med* 1967 **277:** 1329–36.

Pohl R, Yeragani VK, Balon R et al. Isoproterenol induced panic attacks. *Biol Psychiatry* 1988; **24:** 891–902.

Pollack MH, Otto MW, Rosenbaum JF et al. Longitudinal course of panic disorder: findings from the Massachusetts General Hospital Naturalistic Study. *J Clin Psychiatry* 1990; **51**(12, suppl A): 12–16.

Pollack MH, Otto MW. Long-term course and outcome of panic disorder *J Clin Psychiatry* 1997; **58**(suppl. 2): 57–60.

Pollack MH, Smoller JW. The longitudinal course and outcome of panic disorder. *Psych Clin N America* 1995; **18:** 785–801.

Pollack MH, Otto MW, Sabatino S et al. Relationship of childhood anxiety to adult panic disorder: correlates and influence on course. *Am J Psychiatry* 1996; **153:** 376–81.

Pollack MH, Worthington JJ III, Otto MW et al. Venlafaxine for panic disorder: results from a double-blind, placebo-controlled study. *Psychopharmacol Bull* 1996; **32:** 667–70.

Pollack MH, Otto MW, Worthington JJ et al. Sertraline in the treatment of panic disorder: a flexible-dose multicenter trial. *Arch Gen Psychiatry* 1998; **55:** 1010–16.

Ramos RT, Gentil V, Gorenstein C. Clomipramine and initial worsening in panic disorder. *J Psychopharmacol* 1993; **7:** 265–9.

Rapaport MH, Pollack MH, Wolkow R et al. Is placebo response the same as drug response in panic disorder? *Am J Psychiatry* 2000; **157:** 1014–16.

Ravaris CL, Friedman MJ, Hauri PJ, McHugo GJ. A controlled study of alprazolam and propranolol in panic-disordered and agoraphobic outpatients. *J Clin Psychopharmacol* 1991; **11:** 344–50.

Regier DA, Rae DS, Narrow WE et al. Prevalence of anxiety disorders and their comorbidity with mood and addictive disorders; *Br J Psychiatry* 1998; **173**(suppl 34): 24–8.

Reschle AH, Mannuzza S, Chapman TF et al. Sodium lactate response and familial risk for panic disorder. *Am J Psychiatry* 1995 **152:** 277–9.

Rickels K, Schweizer EE. Benzodiazepines for treatment of panic attacks. *Psychopharmacol Bull* 1986; **22:** 93–9.

Robins LN, Helzer JE, Croughan JL. The NIMH diagnostic interview schedule: its history, characteristics, and validity. *Arch Gen Psychiatry* 1981; **38:** 381–9.

Rosenberg R. Treatment of panic disorder with tricyclics and MAOIs. In: Nutt DJ, Ballenger JC, Lepine J-P, eds, *Panic Disorder. Clinical diagnosis, management and mechanisms*. London: Martin Dunitz,1999: 125–44.

Roy-Byrne PP, Cowley DS. Course and outcome in panic disorder: a review of recent follow-up studies. *Anxiety* 1994/1995; **1:** 151–60.

Roy-Byrne PP, Stein MB, Russo J et al. Panic disorder in the primary care setting: comorbidity, disability, service utilisation, and treatment. *J Clin Psychiatry* 1999; **60:** 492–9.

Roy-Byrne PP, Stang P, Wittchen H-U et al. Lifetime panic-depression comorbidity in the National Comorbidity Survey. *Br J Psychiatry* 2000; **176:** 229–35.

Royal Collogo of Psychiatrists. *Benzodiazepines: Risks, benefits or dependence.* RCPsych Council Report 59: London: Royal College of Psychiatrists, 1997.

Salvador-Carulla L, Segui J, Fernandez-Cano P, Canet J. Costs and offset effect in panic disorders. *Br J Psychiatry* 1995; **166**(suppl 27): 23–8.

Sargant W, Dally P. Treatment of anxiety states by antidepressant drugs. *BMJ* 1962; **1:** 6–9.

Schneier FR, Garfinkel R, Kennedy B et al. Ondansetron in the treatment of panic disorder. *Anxiety* 1996; **2:** 199–202.

Schuckit MA, Hesselbrock V. Alcohol dependence and anxiety disorders: what is the relationship? *Am J Psychiatry* 1994; **151:** 1723–34.

Schweizer E, Rickels K, Case G, Greenblatt DJ. long-term therapeutic use of benzodiazepines: II. Effects of gradual taper. *Arch Gen Psychiatry* 1990; **47:** 908–15.

Schweizer E, Rickels K, Weiss S, Zavodnick S. Maintenance drug treatment of panic disorder. I. Results of a prospective, placebo-controlled comparison of alprazolam and imipramine. *Arch Gen Psychiatry* 1993; **50:** 51–60.

Scupi BS, Benson BE, Brown LB, Uhde TW. Rapid onset: a valid panic disorder criterion? *Depr Anxiety* 1997; **5:** 121–26.

Seligman MEP. Competing theories in panic. In: Rachman S, Maser JD, eds, *Panic, Psychological Perspectives.* Hillsdale, NJ: Lawrence Erlbaum, 1988: 321–9.

Shear MK, Cooper AM, Klerman GL et al. A psychodynamic model of panic disorder. *Am J Psychiatry* 1993; **150:** 859–66.

Sheehan DV, Raj AB, Harnett-Sheehan K et al. The relative efficacy of high-dose buspirone and alprazolam in the treatment of panic disorder: a double-blind placebo-controlled study. *Acta Psychiat Scandina* 1993; **88:** 1–11.

Shinoda N, Kodama K, Sakamoto T et al. Predictors of 1-year outcome for patients with panic disorder. *Compr Psychiatry* 1999; **40:** 39–43.

Silverstein B. Gender differences in the prevalence of clinical depression: the role played by depression associated with somatic symptoms. *Am J Psychiatry* 1999; **156**: 480–2.

Spiegel DA, Bruce TJ, Gregg SF, Nuzzarello A. Does cognitive therapy assist slow-taper alprazolam discontinuation in panic disorder. *Am J Psychiatry* 1994 **151**: 876–81.

Stahl SM. Mixed depression and anxiety: Serotonin 1A receptors as a common pharmacologic link. *J Clin Psychiatry* 1997; **58**(suppl 8): 20–6.

Stein MB, Walker JR, Anderson G et al. Childhood physical abuse in patients with anxiety disorders and in a community sample. *Am J Psychiatry* 1996; **153**: 275–7.

Tesar GE, Rosenbaum JF, Pollack MH et al. Double-blind, placebo-controlled comparison of clonazepam and alprazolam for panic disorder. *J Clin Psychiatry* 1991; **52**: 69–76.

Tiller JW, Bouwer C, Behnke K. Moclobemide for anxiety disorders: a focus on moclobemide for panic disorder. *Int Clin Psychopharmacol* 1997; **12**(suppl 6): s27–30.

Tiller JW, Bouwer C, Behnke K. Moclobemide and fluoxetine for panic disorder. *Eur Arch Psychiatry Clin Neurosc* 1999; **249**(suppl 1): S7–10.

Torgersen S. Genetic factors in anxiety disorders. *Arch Gen Psychiatry* 1983; **40**: 1085–9.

Townsend MH, Bologna NB, Barbee JG. Heart rate and blood pressure in panic disorder, major depression, and comorbid panic disorder with major depression. *Psychiat Res* 1998; **79**: 187–90.

Tweed JL, Schoebach VJ, George LK, Blazer DG. The effects of childhood parental death and divorce on six-month history of anxiety disorders. *Br J Psychiatry* 1989; **154**: 823–8.

Tyrer P. *Classification of Neurosis*. Chichester: John Wiley & Sons, 1984.

Udhe TW, Stein MB, Vittone BJ et al. Behavioral and physiologic effects of short-term and long-term administration of clonidine in panic disorder. *Arch Gen Psychiatry* 1989; **46**: 170–7.

van Balkom AJLM, van Dyck R. Comments on the APA panic disorder guideline. *Am J Psychiatry* 1998; **155**: 1798.

van Balkom AJLM, Bakker A, Spinhoven PH et al. A meta-analysis of the treatment of panic disorder with or without agoraphobia: a comparison of psychopharmacological, cognitive–behavioral, and combination treatments. *J Nerv Ment Dis* 1997; **185:** 510–16.

Wade AG, Lepola U, Koponen HJ et al. The effect of citalopram in panic disorder. *Br J Psychiatry* 1997; **170:** 549–53.

Walker EA, Katon WJ, Jemelka RP, Roy-Byrne PP. Comorbidity of gastrointestinal complaints, depression and anxiety in the Epidemiological Catchment Area Study. *Am J Med* 1992; **92:** S26–30.

Wardle J, Hayward P, Higgit A et al. Effects of concurrent diazepam treatment on the outcome of exposure therapy in agoraphobia. *Behav Res Therapy* 1994; **32:** 203–15.

Weise RE, Shear MK, Maser JD. On the need for standardisation in panic disorder treatment research: survey of the literature 1980-1992. *Anxiety* 1996; **2:** 257–64.

Weisman MM, Markovitz JS, Ouellette R et al. Panic disorder and cardiovascular and cerebrovascular problems: results from a community survey. *Am J Psychiatry* 1990; **147:** 1504–8.

Weissman MM, Bland RC, Canino GJ et al. The Cross-national epidemiology of panic disorder. *Arch Gen Psychiatry* 1997; **54:** 305–9.

Wells K, Stewart K, Hays R et al. The functioning and well-being of depressed patients: the results of the Medical Outcome Study. *JAMA* 1989; **262:** 914–19.

Wittchen H-U. What is comorbidity – fact or artefact? Br J Psychiatry 1996a; **168**(suppl 30): 7–8.

Wittchen H-U. Critical issues in the evaluation of co-morbidity of psychiatric disorders. *Br J Psychiatry* 1996b; **168**(suppl 30), 9–16

Wolpe J, Rowan VC. Panic disorders: a product of classical conditioning. *Behav Res Therapy* 1988; **26:** 441–50.

World Health Organization. *International Classification of Mental and Behavioural Disorders: Clinical descriptions and diagnostic guidelines*, 10th revision. Geneva: WHO, 1992.

Worthington JJ III, Pollack MH, Otto MW et al. Long-term experience with clonazepam in patients with a primary diagnosis of panic disorder. *Psychopharmacol Bull* 1998; **34:** 199–205.

Yonkers KA, Zlotnick C, Allsworth J et al. Is the course of panic disorder the same in women and men? *Am J Psychiatry* 1998; **155:** 596–602.

Index